Murder Most Vile
Volume 25

18 Truly Shocking
Murder Cases

Robert Keller

**Please Leave Your Review of This Book at
http://bit.ly/kellerbooks**

ISBN: 9781093797565

Table of Contents

Appointment with a Killer

Scott Singleton

Lynne Rogers was a determined young woman. Recently laid off from an administrative job, the 17-year-old had launched a concerted effort to find new employment. And her goal was not just any old job but the kind that she yearned for, one that offered the chance of international travel. And so, Lynne had spent weeks scouring business directories, eventually coming up with a list of over 300 companies in and around London. She'd then written to all of them, enclosing her résumé and details of the kind of position she was interested in. To her surprise and delight, she'd received a personal reply within days. The man who called said that he was the owner of a company that jetted high-level executives to and from Europe. He was looking for qualified young women who could perform secretarial duties on these trips. The pay on offer was £14,000 per annum, more than double what Lynne had earned at her previous job. Was she interested? Of course she was.

Despite the misgivings of her father and sister, Lynne was over the moon about the potential job offer. In the days leading up to her scheduled interview, she had her hair styled and sent her most practical outfit to the dry cleaners. She also borrowed a typewriter from a friend and spent an entire weekend honing up on her less-than-adequate typing skills. On the morning of September 4, 1991, she was a bag of nerves. Her potential employer had called again the previous day and told her to meet him at Charing Cross station in central London. He'd told her that they would be driving to Shoreham-by-Sea in West Sussex and taking a helicopter from there to Gatwick Airport. He also told her to bring her passport along. It sounded almost too good to be true – and it was.

On September 4, Lynne Rogers bade her father, Derek, and her older sister, Suzanne, goodbye. She told them that she would call as soon as she knew the outcome of the interview. Then she boarded the train at Catford, London bound for Charing Cross. Her family would never see her alive again.

By 10:00 that night, Derek Rogers was becoming concerned. He knew that Lynne had taken her passport with her and that her new employer might well have taken her on a day-trip to the continent. But he also knew his daughter. Lynne was a diligent, reliable girl. She'd promised to call and she would definitely have done so had she been able. After waiting a half-hour more, Derek went to the Catford police station and reported her missing.

The missing persons case was assigned to Detective Superintendent Douglas Auld. But as the days passed with no clue as to Lynne's whereabouts, it became increasingly clear that something bad had happened to her. Soon the story was attracting massive attention in the British media. Teenaged girls do not simply vanish from the busy streets of London in broad daylight, at least not unseen.

The first clue to Lynne's disappearance emerged when a man came forward to report a strange conversation he'd overheard. According to the witness, he'd been making a call from a public telephone in Crawley, Sussex, in the days before Lynne went missing. In the call box next to him was a man who was talking quite loudly. The witness could hear everything that was said, and he found the conversation to be odd. The was talking about a job offer involving international travel. He also mentioned a helicopter ride during the interview process. What the witness found strange was that such a lucrative offer would be made via public telephone. He also noticed that the man had a small tape recorder which he held up to receiver throughout the conversation. After reading about Lynne's disappearance in the newspaper, the witness had decided to come forward with what he'd heard. Unfortunately, he could not give a description of the man he'd seen, and the call box itself yielded no clues. Hundreds of callers had since handled the phone, obliterating any fingerprints.

On September 9, five days after the disappearance, the investigation took a dramatic turn when the body of a young girl was found hidden in dense undergrowth in Rotherfield, Sussex, some 40 miles south of London. It was Lynne Rogers and she had been brutally strangled.

The location at which the body had been found meant that the murder inquiry was conducted by the Sussex Police, with Detective Superintendent Michael Bennison taking charge. Initially, the belief was that this was a sex crime, but the subsequent autopsy threw up a surprise when it revealed that Lynne had not been sexually assaulted. There were, however, curious bruises on her chin which would turn out, on closer inspection, to be tooth impressions. Since bite marks are as unique as fingerprints, this was a valuable clue.

But it would only be of value if the police could find someone to match the bite against, and at this point they had no idea who might have done this or why. Speaking to Lynne's sister Suzanne, they learned that the mysterious caller had phoned four times and that Suzanne had spoken to him once, when Lynne was out. She said that she had heard airplanes and flight announcements in the background. Did this mean that some of the killer's cover story was true, that he was an airline employee?

Further support for this theory came which police got a call from another witness, London cab driver Thomas Reynolds. According to Reynolds, he had been parked outside Charing Cross station on the morning of September 4 and had seen Lynne Rogers, noticing her because she was an attractive redhead. Then a blue car had pulled up, driven by a man in a pilot's uniform. Lynne had exchanged a greeting with the man and had then walked around to the passenger door and gotten in. Moments later, the car had pulled away from the curb and blended into the traffic, most likely taking Lynne to her death. The cabbie did not take note of the vehicle's license plate number, but he did know that it was a Vauxhall Carlton.

In the meantime, the police had been working another angle. The killer had quite obviously obtained Lynne's contact details from one of the letters she'd sent to potential employers. A list of those 319 companies had been found in Lynne's bedroom and, initially, the police thought they'd have to undertake the considerable task of contacting all of them. But then Suzanne remembered something that the caller had told her during their brief conversation. He'd mentioned that he'd gotten Lynne's CV from a company based in Greenwich, south London. Only one of the companies on the list was in that locale, an organization called Africa Hinterland.

That company, detectives soon discovered, had gone out of business even before Lynne had written to them. But it turned out that they still received mail at the business park where they'd once had premises. That mail was placed in a general mailbox at the park, along with items addressed to other former tenants. This is where Lynne's résumé would have ended up.

But who would have been able to access it there? Anyone who'd formerly rented premises at the park, according to the facilities manager. He was then asked whether any of those former tenants drove a blue Vauxhall Carlton; and said that there was someone, a man named Wayne Scott Singleton who had owned a now defunct operation called Casualty Car Doctor. The park manager also added that Singleton was from Crawley. The call summoning Lynne to her fateful interview had, of course, been made from that area.

Wayne Scott Singleton was now the main suspect in the murder of Lynne Rogers. Looking into his background, investigators learned that he was a married father of two who was separated from his wife and currently involved with a long-term girlfriend. But that told only a part of the story. It turned out that the suspect had a long police record for petty crime and that Singleton was not even his real name. He had been born Andre Reich. Another interesting detail was that Singleton was obsessed with flying, claimed to be a trained pilot, and often wore a pilot's uniform. He'd even convinced his wife and girlfriend that he was qualified to fly light passenger aircraft.

On September 28, the police launched a coordinated operation, simultaneously raiding several addresses where they thought Singleton might be. Taken into custody, an outraged Singleton vociferously protested his innocence. He even expressed sympathy for Lynne's family and expressed his hope that the killer would soon be caught. However, when the police asked him to let them take a dental impression in order to eliminate him as a suspect, Singleton flatly refused. With nothing but circumstantial evidence against him, the police were only able to hold him for 36 hours and were then forced to let him go.

A few days after Singleton's release, the police received a tip from a Rotherfield farmer named Richard Ellis, who reported that had seen a blue Vauxhall parked beside the road close to where Lynne's body was found. This had occurred on September 4, the very day that the young woman disappeared. More importantly, Ellis had written down the license plate number. He'd recently suffered acts of vandalism on his farm, he said, and had jotted down the number for future reference. Now he handed over that number to the police. They ran it through the system. It belonged to Scott Singleton who had recently told the police that he'd never been to Rotherfield and didn't even know where it was.

This was once again a valuable lead. But the police did not want to make the mistake again of jumping the gun. What they really needed was that impression of Singleton's teeth and since he was refusing to cooperate on that score, they were going to have to do it the hard way. Teams of detectives began working the areas surrounding Singleton's home, his wife's home, his girlfriend's home. Eventually, their persistence and hard work paid off when they tracked down a dentist who had done dental work on Singleton. As chance would have it, he still had a plaster impression of Singleton's teeth. That was handed to a forensic odontologist who compared it to the bite marks on the victim and was emphatic in his opinion that only Scott Singleton could have inflicted those injuries.

On October 10, 1991, Wayne Scott Singleton was re-arrested and charged with the murder of Lynne Rogers. The case against him appeared overwhelming, but still the prosecution was worried about two issues. The first was that Singleton's girlfriend was still providing him with an alibi; the second was that this was a crime without an apparent motive. Juries have been known to acquit when the prosecutor fails to explain why the victim was killed.

So why had Lynne Rogers been murdered. If it wasn't rape or robbery and if her killer had never even met her before the day she was killed, then why? The clue may be hidden hidden deep in the warped psyche of Scott Singleton. Forensic psychiatrists who have examined the case believe that Singleton had staged the whole episode in order to seduce Lynne. He had attempted to impress her with his alter-ego as a handsome pilot but had been rebuffed. An ego as fragile as Singleton's does not take rejection well. It had sent him into a murderous rage during which he had snuffed out the life of a beautiful young woman who had only wanted to create a better life for herself.

Singleton's alibi also would not stand the test of time. At trial, his girlfriend, Kim, decided to change sides and testify for the prosecution. Called to give evidence, she admitted that she had lied about Singleton being with her at the time of the murder. She also handed over a cassette tape to the police. On it was a recording of airplane engines and a voice giving take-off instructions to various aircraft. This was the tape that Singleton had played in the background while talking to Lynne and to her sister.

Wayne Scott Singleton a.k.a. Andre Reich was found guilty of murder and sentenced to life in prison with a minimum term of 15 years. This was a ridiculously lenient sentence for such a callous murder, and it was just too much for Lynne's father to take. "Is that all?" Derek Rogers shouted at the judge. "After what he's done to me, my family, my daughter, you put him away 15 years." He then lunged for Singleton and had to be restrained by court officials. It is easy to understand his pain. The man who had taken away his precious daughter will one day walk free. And he will always be a danger to women.

Empty Words

Ann Kontz

Lieutenant Chris Morgan was an old-school detective, right down to the fedora hat he often wore, making him look like an extra in a Humphrey Bogart movie. And like the character Sam Spade, so memorably portrayed by Bogart in *The Maltese Falcon*, Morgan was tenacious, a dog with a bone once he had a puzzle to solve. Still, Morgan had never encountered an investigation quite like the Eric Miller case.

Miller had been a scientist, a pediatric AIDS researcher at the University of North Carolina at Chapel Hill. He was happily married to Ann, who he'd met while both of them were students at Purdue University. Ann had a successful career, too. She was a chemist at a large pharmaceutical company in Raleigh, North Carolina, where the couple had their home. When baby Clare was born in 2000, Eric was over the moon, besotted with his daughter and looking forward to the role he would play in her life. Eric, though, would not live to see his daughter grow up. Within a year of her birth, he would be dead.

It started during a bowling night on November 15, 2000. Eric had gone to the AMF Pleasant Valley Lanes in Raleigh with Derril Willard, a co-worker of his wife Ann and an acquaintance of both of them. During the evening, he'd consumed a beer, brought to him by Willard, and complained that it tasted bitter. After returning home, he'd become violently ill and had been rushed to hospital. There, doctors diagnosed him with a bad case of flu and kept him on bed rest and intravenous fluids. That stabilized his condition and within a couple of days he was well enough to go home.

But just a week later, Eric was back in the hospital with similar, although more severe, symptoms. This time doctors ran some tests and were shocked to discover high levels of arsenic in his body. Emergency measures were called for and managed to stabilize him. Then, just when it appeared that he might pull through, he took a sudden and inexplicable turn for the worse. Within hours of his diagnosis, Eric Miller was dead.

The Raleigh Police were, of course, called in to investigate. This was, after all, a case of poisoning. But the initial impression was that Eric had ingested the arsenic accidentally. A search was, therefore, carried out at the Miller home and at Eric's workplace, looking for the source of the poison. It turned up nothing that could account for the levels of arsenic in Eric's body. And if accidental poisoning was ruled out, that left only one other possibility. Murder.

It was at this point that Lt. Morgan entered the investigation. And the first question that the veteran detective had to answer was the obvious one – motive. Who might have wanted the well-liked and respected scientist dead? Had Eric Miller had any enemies? Maybe a professional rival? Had he been involved in anything shady? An illicit affair, perhaps? Maybe his wife would have some idea.

But Ann Miller was so grief-stricken that she was barely able to speak, let alone answer questions. She clung to her father for the duration of the interview and periodically broke into uncontrollable sobs. It was pitiful to watch and Morgan eventually called an end to the interview without having learned anything new.

Morgan's next move was to trace the history of Eric Miller's mysterious illness. By all accounts, Eric had first displayed symptoms after his bowling night with Derril Willard, and so Morgan decided to bring Willard in for questioning. But Willard proved a difficult man to pin down. He was never available and all phone messages went unanswered. Then, while still trying to pin the man down to an interview, Morgan received an intriguing piece of information. One of Willard's work colleagues told him that Willard was infatuated with Ann Miller. Could that, perhaps, have been a motive for murder?

Looking into Willard's background, Morgan found that he was a respected biochemist, 37 years of age, married, with a baby daughter. The marriage was apparently a happy one. But when the police started delving into Willard's phone records, a different picture emerged. There was one number that appeared more than any other, and that number belonged to none other than Ann Miller. Multiple calls passed between them every day, including one made at 4:30 a.m. Why, Morgan wondered, would someone need to call a co-worker at 4:30 in the morning?

The answer to that question emerged when the detective discovered that Willard and Miller had taken a trip to Chicago together in late November. Supposedly, it was a business trip, although their employer knew nothing about it. Turns out, they had checked into a suite at the Ritz Carlton and remained indoors for the entire weekend, living off room service. If that wasn't proof of an affair between the two of them, Morgan discovered e-mails on Ann Miller's computer which left him in no doubt. "I never want to stop making you feel," Ann had written to her lover. "I want to show you new things. I want to touch places in you that you never knew existed."

By now, Morgan was considering two possibilities. Either Willard had murdered Eric to rid himself of a love rival, or the lovers had conspired together to kill the man who stood between them. The grieving widow might have been able to resolve the issue, but Ann Miller had now hired a lawyer and was refusing to speak to the police.

As for Derril Willard, Morgan had eventually tracked him down, although Derril was also insistent on having his lawyer present during any interrogation. It would be the last time that Morgan ever spoke to him. Within 24 hours came the shocking news that Willard was dead. His wife had found his lifeless body in the garage beside a suicide note. "The world looks black to me," he had written. "All I can see is the smearing of my name, pain caused to my family, personal humiliation and probable economic ruin. I have been accused of an action for which I am not responsible. I have taken no one's life save my own."

Willard's family was, of course, devastated by his death. In its aftermath, his wife Yvette told the police that he had admitted his affair with Ann but had always denied involvement in Eric's murder. "He wasn't capable of murder," Yvette said. "He would have encouraged Ann to get a divorce, not help her kill her husband."

Derril Willard's death was a serious setback to the investigation, but it was a boon to Ann Miller. All along, she been spinning a story to her late husband's family, painting Willard as the villain of the piece. "He's obsessed with me," she had told them. "He probably believed that we could be together if Eric was out of the way."

Convincing though she was, it was incredibly naive of Ann to think that evidence of her deceit would not come to light. Aside from the trail of telephone calls, e-mails, and hotel bookings, there were the forensics. As a scientist, she should have known that arsenic is one of the easiest poisons to detect. Analysis of Eric's hair showed that the poisoning had started four months before the night he became ill at the bowling alley. That meant that he had been fed small doses over a long period of time, and who but his wife had the access required to carry that out. The M.E. also discovered that he had been given a fatal dose on the day he died. Incredible though it seems, someone had snuck into Eric's hospital room and finished him off with a final helping of arsenic. The person who could do such a thing had to be incredibly cold and calculating, in fact, a psychopath.

To Morgan, that explained Ann's histrionics in the aftermath of her husband's death, her near collapse at his funeral; it explained her lack of remorse after her lover's suicide; it explained her ability to so utterly dupe the family of her victim. It also explained how she could leave town so soon after Eric's death, moving 120 miles away to

Wilmington and starting up a relationship there with a new man, a musician named Paul Kontz.

At this point, Ann probably thought that she had gotten away with murder. And with the District Attorney stalling over bringing charges, it seemed that she may be right. The problem was with establishing a clear trail of evidence. No one could place the arsenic in Ann Miller's hands. Without that key connection, Miller's high-profile lawyers would sweep the floor with any prosecutor. Miller would be acquitted, and the Double Jeopardy rule would mean that she could never be tried again. The D.A. wasn't about to take that risk, and so the matter sat for a year, going nowhere despite Lieutenant Morgan going over the case files for what felt like a hundred times.

Then, in early 2002, Morgan was again reviewing the files when he stumbled on something so obvious that he couldn't believe that he hadn't picked it up before. It was contained within the transcript of an interview that the police had conducted with Derril Willard's wife. Yvette Willard had told the police that Derril had visited his lawyer, Rick Gammon, on the day prior to his death. During that meeting, Gammon had apparently warned Willard that he might be charged with attempted murder. And why would Gammon have told him that? There could only be one reason. Willard had revealed something to Gammon, something that directly related to Eric Miller's death, something that the police did not know about yet.

There was a problem, though. Despite Willard's death, attorney-client privilege still applied. Gammon was not required to reveal the information. Indeed, he was barred from doing so. The only way around it was an order from a judge. The outcome of the case and justice for Eric Miller and the Miller family hinged on it.

The court battle to obtain access to Gammon's files would be a protracted one, enduring for three years. During that time, Ann Miller wed her musician boyfriend, Paul Kontz, and Lt. Chris Morgan put off his retirement by a year so that he could follow the Miller case through to the end. He was determined to see justice done.

In the spring of 2004, Morgan's persistence was finally rewarded when the North Carolina Supreme Court ordered Gammon to reveal what Derril Willard had told him about Eric Miller's murder. The revelation was just as shocking as Morgan had expected it would be. According to Willard, Ann Miller had admitted to him that she had injected arsenic into Eric's IV bag while he lay in his hospital bed. This was the "final, fatal dose" that the medical examiner had spoken of.

Ann Kontz was arrested and charged with her former husband's murder. Capital punishment is an option in North Carolina, and the D.A. must have been tempted to push for it in a case as aggravated as this one. In the end, though, he decided that it was too risky. Ann, with her well-rehearsed histrionics, might just be able to sway a jury. Instead, the D.A. offered a plea bargain – 25 to 31 years in prison, the maximum for a first offender. With a life sentence as the likely alternative, Ann's attorney advised her to take the deal.

In November 2005, Ann Kontz stood before a judge in a North Carolina courtroom and admitted that she had murdered Eric Miller.

Her attorney then read a prepared statement in which she expressed remorse for what she'd done. "Empty words" was how Eric's father described them.

So why did Ann Kontz murder her husband? Why not just divorce him if she was unhappy with her marriage and wanted to be with someone else? Kontz offered no explanation for her actions, but Lieutenant Morgan has a theory that rings true.

"She couldn't divorce him," Morgan said, "because that amounts to admitting that she's not perfect. So instead she kills him. That would mean that she is looked at by her friends as this total victim."

Ann Kontz will remain behind bars until at least 2029. She will be 59 years old before she is eligible for parole.

Pure Evil

Sylvia Fleming was 17 years old and she was in love. The object of her affection, a part-time fireman named Stephen Scott, was nine years older than Sylvia, but that in no way distracted from her feelings for him. Stephen understood teenagers. In fact, his apartment at Lisanelly Heights in Omagh, Northern Ireland, was a haven for them. There were always teens hanging out, smoking, drinking and listening while Stephen held court. They regarded the short, thickset bodybuilder, known locally by the nickname Bulldog, as somewhat of a hero. Sylvia thought of him in those terms, too. After meeting him at a party at his apartment in December 1997, she was instantly besotted. When he began paying attention to her, she was beside herself. When he tempted her into his bed and when they then started dating, she thought she was in heaven.

Sylvia's sisters, Josie and Kathleen, were not so sure. They wanted the best for their little sister, of course they did. They just did not think that the brash, boastful Scott was a safe bet. Sylvia had already been through so much in her short life.

Placed into care after their single father was no longer able to look
after them, the girls had been passed from one foster home to the next.
They had been lucky enough to stay together during that time, but all
of them, including Sylvia, had suffered physical and emotional abuse
along the way. It had cemented a unique bond between the sisters.
They looked after one another, and right now oldest sister Josie felt it
was her duty to warn Sylvia to take things slowly with Scott.

Sylvia, of course, wasn't listening. Desperate for affection, she
accepted Scott's offer to move into his apartment when he asked.
Then, another side of him began to emerge. He began to become more
and more controlling, systematically isolating her from her sisters and
other friends. He began to become physically and mentally abusive,
belittling her at every turn, even in front of others. Sylvia also learned
that he had an obsession with serial killers, especially with Ted Bundy,
who he appeared to idolize. In bed, he began to become violent
towards her, objectifying her during sex, humiliating her, insisting on
tying her up, once even trying to suffocate her. Sylvia took all of this
abuse because, despite everything he had done to her, she loved
Stephen. And somewhere in his heart, she was certain that he loved
her.

Then came the day in March 1998 that Sylvia discovered that she was
pregnant. She was fearful of telling Scott, fearful of what his response
might be. And she was right to be afraid. Scott was furious. He denied
that the child was his and accused her of sleeping around. Eventually,
he said that he wanted to end the relationship, and a tearful Sylvia
moved out of the apartment and into shared accommodation with a
friend.

The break-up came as a relief to Josie and Kathleen. For a while, it appeared that their little sister was back to her old feisty self. Sylvia got a job at a care home for the elderly, while she continued her studies to become a hairdresser. But then, Scott was back. Reluctant to relinquish control over Sylvia, he began sweet-talking his way back into his affections. Sylvia, of course, still loved him, and soon she was back in his bed, allowing herself to be tied up and humiliated.

On Friday, April 3, 1998, Sylvia proudly showed her housemate her first paycheck from the care home. The girls spent the early part of that evening together before Sylvia said that she was going over to Stephen Scott's apartment and would be spending the night. That was just before eleven, and the walk would have taken Sylvia around fifteen minutes. She could not have known that she was walking herself to her death.

Scott had company when Sylvia arrived, a boy and a girl, both 14. That, however, was not unusual, and Sylvia thought nothing of it. She went with Scott into the bedroom when he asked her and accepted the glass of wine he pushed into her hand, not knowing that he had doped it with sleeping pills. After just a few sips, she began to feel drowsy, and that was when Scott pinned her to the bed, tied her up and placed duct tape over her eyes and mouth. Already woozy, Sylvia must have felt like she was being suffocated. But the worst was yet to come. While she lay helpless on the bed, the man she loved injected her with insulin.

The effect of insulin to a person who does not have diabetes, is profound. It significantly lowers the blood sugar and, depending on the dosage, may induce coma or even cause death. We don't know for sure whether this was how Sylvia Fleming was killed, but we do know that Stephen Scott lingered a long time with her before calling in the two 14-year-olds. Earlier in the evening, before Sylvia arrived, Scott had told them that he was going to kill her. Now, looking down at the bound and gagged corpse, they realized that they'd been wrong to take his comment as an empty boast. "You're in this now," he told them. "Both of you." He then instructed the boy to help him move the body into the attic. Then, in an act of barely believable indifference, he took £25 from Sylvia's purse, the money she was so proud to have earned, and took the teenagers swimming at the local leisure center.

By Saturday afternoon, Sylvia's housemate was getting worried about her. She called Josie and Kathleen, and together the three of them went to Scott's flat. There, an obviously agitated Scott told them that he hadn't seen or heard from Sylvia and quickly hustled them out of the door. As they were leaving, Josie noticed some rucksacks lined up against the wall. Little did she know that those bags contained the butchered remains of her sister. After returning from the leisure center, Scott had dragged Sylvia's body to the bathroom and lifted her into the tub. Then he'd got to work, dismembering her with a hacksaw, removing the head and arms, the legs below the knee and the thighs. These had been packed into garbage bags and then stowed in the backpacks. Now, certain that Josie would go to the police, Scott summoned his 14-year-old accomplice to help him get rid of the body.

While Sylvia's family and friends hit the streets looking for her, Scott and his accomplice made their way across town, carrying their rucksacks. Their destination was a new housing development, where there were freshly dug foundations. This was where Scott planned to bury the remains, thinking no doubt that the trenches would soon be filled with concrete, hiding his gruesome secret forever. Later that night, he'd visit another part of the development, this time in the company of a 21-year-old friend, to dispose of the rest of the remains.

Two weeks after Sylvia's disappearance, Stephen Scott was asked to come down to police headquarters to answer questions about her whereabouts. He vociferously denied having anything to do with it and willingly agreed to a search of his apartment. That search was carried out right away. It yielded nothing that the police considered incriminating. The police, in fact, told Josie that they believed Sylvia had run away.

But Scott's habit of involving others in his nefarious deeds was about to come back to haunt him. On May 13, 1998, Scott's 21-year-old accomplice was arrested in Omagh on unrelated charges. Desperate to avoid jail time, he offered to tell detectives about Sylvia's murder in exchange for charges against him being dropped. He then repeated what Scott had told him about the murder and led officers to the spot where he and Scott had buried some of the remains. These were so badly decomposed that Sylvia could only be identified from dental records.

Steve Scott and the two 14-year-olds were immediately arrested. Meanwhile, news of the gruesome discovery had spilled out, sparking a furious response from the citizens of Omagh. Rioting broke out and would continue for three days during which the homes of those involved were firebombed by angry mobs.

Meanwhile, Scott was being subjected to a fierce round of interrogation. Initially, he denied any involvement in Sylvia's death.

Then, confronted by evidence that bone and skin fragments matching Sylvia's DNA had been found in the drains of his apartment, he changed his story. He now admitted giving Sylvia sleeping pills and tying her up. However, he insisted that it was all part of a sex game and that he hadn't harmed her. According to him, he'd left the room and had returned to find the 14-year-old boy strangling Sylvia. Realizing that she was dead, he'd panicked and decided to dispose of the body.

The police didn't believe one word of Scott's story, and neither did the jury at his trial. Found guilty of murder and of the unlawful disposal of a corpse, he was sentenced to life in prison with a minimum tariff of 19 years. Of his accomplices, the 21-year-old man and the 14-year-old boy each got two-and-a-half years. The girl was acquitted on all charges.

The 19-year minimum tariff seemed to most observers to be a particularly lenient sentence, especially in a trial where the testimony had driven several in the gallery, including members of the press corps, to tears. All that Sylvia's grieving family could hope for was that Scott would not be released after serving the minimum, that he would spend the rest of his natural life behind bars. Alas, it was not to be. By 2015, Scott was receiving weekend furloughs in preparation for his release. By 2017, the man who had been described by his trial judge as "pure evil" was back on the streets.

Bad Candy

Cordelia Botkin

John Preston Dunning had lived an interesting life. A seasoned war correspondent with the Associated Press, Dunning had spent years traveling the globe to cover various conflicts. A daredevil by nature, he enjoyed getting right where the action was and damn the risk. This, of course, imbued his writing with a sense of immediacy and made him a sought-after journalist. And Dunning's larger-than-life persona extended to his personal life, too. When he wasn't working, John could be found drinking, gambling and chasing women. It was a wonder that his wife, Mary, put up with it. And yet she did. Despite his indiscretions, Mary was devoted to John and to their baby daughter.

Then, in 1892, there was respite for the long-suffering Mary Dunning, at last. John had been appointed to run the Associated Press West Coast bureau, a placement that took the family to San Francisco. John's globetrotting days were over and with them, Mary hoped, his philandering ways. But that was a forlorn wish. Shortly after the family settled into the Bay area, John was cycling through Golden Gate Park when the chain slipped from his bicycle. As he crouched down to address the problem, he spotted a woman sitting on a nearby bench. She was somewhat heavy-set and far from conventionally attractive. Looks, however, had never been a major consideration to John Dunning. Conquest was what mattered. He struck up a conversation with the woman and then started flirting openly with her. By the time his bicycle was back in working order, he had secured a date.

Like John Dunning, Cordelia Botkin had seen her fair share of what the world had to offer. At 41, she was ten years older than John and currently married to Welcome A. Botkin, a wealthy businessman from Stockton, California. Although they were separated, Botkin still supported his wife financially, allowing Cordelia to live a life of leisure. That leisure time was spent at the kind of activities that John Dunning so enjoyed. Cordelia was well acquainted with the seedier side of San Francisco, to its gambling dens, gin joints and bawdy houses. Over the months that followed, she made it her mission to introduce Dunning to her favorite haunts.

To Mary Dunning, the stories that started circulating about her husband's shenanigans with a married, older woman, were difficult to bear. Mary was a somewhat innocent woman, but she wasn't naïve. She was well aware of the kind of man she'd married and, as has already been noted, she'd tolerated John's indiscretions in the past. This, however, was different. This was in the public eye. People were talking. She was being openly humiliated. Eventually she could take it no more and informed her husband that she was moving back to Delaware with their daughter. John barely put up a fight. After seeing Mary off at the Oakland railway station, he packed up his things and moved into Cordelia's room at the Hotel Victoria. Now the party could begin in earnest.

But the problem with such sustained debauchery is that there is eventually a price to be paid. As Dunning's drinking and partying accelerated, he began a headlong descent into alcoholism. At the same time, his gambling debts were mounting, and there were some shady characters making noises about calling in their markers. Desperate, Dunning perpetrated a ham-fisted fraud against his employers, stealing $4,000. This was soon uncovered, resulting in Dunning being fired from his job. He was fortunate that the Associated Press decided not to file charges.

John Dunning, the swash-buckling war correspondent and serial philanderer, was now reduced to being a kept man. Not that Cordelia seemed to mind. She enjoyed having her lover under her control. But this not-so-cozy arrangement wouldn't last. In 1898, the Spanish-American War broke out, offering Dunning a chance at redemption. He might have been a lousy administrator (and a fraudster into the bargain) but the AP knew that he was an excellent writer. They offered him a job covering the conflict. Like a drowning man grasping for a life preserver, Dunning grabbed the opportunity with both hands.

Cordelia didn't want him to go. In fact, she begged him not to go, shedding copious tears in support of her argument. But John's mind was made up. Not only was he taking the job, but he informed Cordelia that he would not be returning to San Francisco when it was over. He was going back to Delaware to be with his wife and child. This revelation left Cordelia stunned, shocked into silence for once. It also left her deeply hurt and, as time went by, hungry for revenge. Dunning had ended affairs with women before, but he'd never known a woman quite like Cordelia Botkin. He had no idea what she was capable of.

During the years that Dunning and his wife had been living apart, he'd
nonetheless kept up a regular correspondence with her. Mary had
always delighted in receiving his letters and had always replied
promptly. Sometimes a letter a day passed between them, always
couched in loving terms, despite their fractured marriage. And Mary
was particularly pleased by the missive she received in September
1898, informing her that John was going back to work and that he
hoped to return to Delaware once his latest assignment was completed.

But a less than agreeable letter arrived in Mary's mailbox that same
day. It was from a confidential "concerned party" who informed Mary
that her husband was currently engaged in a torrid affair with a young
Englishwoman. According to the writer, this woman was currently
"divorcing from her husband, all owing to the marked intimacy with
Mr. Dunning." Mary, who had dealt with such things many times in
the past, decided to ignore it.

A few days later, there was another delivery, a small package this
time, wrapped in plain brown paper and postmarked San Francisco.
Inside was an elegant white box, decorated with a pink ribbon. Across
the top, in gold script was the word "Bonbons." The note that came
with it read: "With love to yourself and baby." It was signed "Mrs. C,"
which Mary assumed was a close friend of hers from California,
Phyllis Corbaley. Once Mary opened the box, she was more certain
than ever that it was from Phyllis. Inside were three rows of fine
chocolate creams, delicately sprinkled with icing sugar. Everyone
close to Mary knew how much she loved candy.

That afternoon, while sitting on the porch enjoying the warm August
sunshine, Mary Dunning produced her box of treats and offered them

around. Mary, her sister Ida Deane, and two of Ida's children each had a piece of candy. So did two young women of Mary's acquaintance, who happened to be passing the house at that time. By that evening, all of them were violently ill with severe stomach cramps and vomiting. All would recover, except for Ida Deane, who died on August 11, and Mary Dunning, who died a day later. Autopsies would reveal that they had ingested large amounts of arsenic.

John Dunning was in Puerto Rico when he received the devastating news of his wife's death. He immediately boarded a ship for New York, arriving to a throng of reporters, firing questions in his direction. The questions directed at him by the police were even more pressing. Had Mary had any enemies? Who might have wanted to harm her? Dunning thought that he might know the answer to those questions. He suggested the name of Cordelia Botkin. That same day, Delaware police sent word to their counterparts in San Francisco, asking them to take Cordelia into custody. They found her at the home of her husband in Stockton, apparently resigned to the fate that awaited her. "The chagrin is past," she told the arresting officers. "The horror is over. I have suffered the humiliation and I am ready."

By the following day, the long distance poisoning (only the second recorded murder by mail in American history) was the biggest news story in the country. Meanwhile, the police were having a hard time building a case against Cordelia. Was the handwriting on the fatal note a match for Cordelia's? One expert said it was, another wasn't certain. Where had the candy and the arsenic been purchased? Despite a city-wide appeal, the San Francisco police were having a hard time finding that out. They could not even say where the package had been mailed from since a recent change to the city's mail sorting protocols made that inconclusive.

There was also the issue of jurisdiction to deal with. Delaware authorities wanted Cordelia to stand trial where the deaths had occurred and applied for her extradition. Cordelia's lawyers fought that motion, correctly asserting that their client had never set foot in the state. They wanted the trial held in California, and in the end, they got their wish. On December 6, 1898, the so-called "trial of the century" got underway.

By the time she appeared for her first day in court, the angst that Cordelia Botkin had displayed at the time of her arrest was long gone. She seemed to be enjoying herself, smiling and posing for the cameras. Even the papers commented on her grandstanding and thirst for publicity. But those smiles would evaporate once the proceedings got underway. The case against her might have been tenuous at first, but dogged police work had turned up some devastating evidence. Detectives had tracked down the confectioner from whom she'd bought the chocolates. They'd also found the chemist who had sold her the arsenic (she'd said she needed it to clean a straw hat). There was also a sales clerk who'd sold her a lace handkerchief, similar to one that had been contained within the package. Cordelia had foolishly posted it with the store label still attached.

And she'd been equally careless in her disposal of evidence. In her room at the Hotel Victoria, the police had found, paper, string, and a seal that had been carefully pried from a candy box. It all added up to a strong circumstantial case. From the moment the evidence was introduced, there was little doubt as to how the trial would go.

On December 30, 1898, the matter went to the jury, which deliberated for four hours before returning a verdict of guilty against Cordelia Botkin for two counts of murder. That verdict might well have sent Cordelia to the gallows. Had it been obtained against a male defendant, there is little doubt that that would have been the outcome. In Cordelia's case, however, the judge opted for the comparative mercy of a life sentence, to be served in the women's ward at San Quentin State Prison.

Cordelia Botkin would remain behind bars for 11 years. During that time, her life seemed to be afflicted by one tragedy after another as her mother, sister, son, and husband died in quick succession. But it was the death of her former lover that affected Cordelia most profoundly. John Dunning had been tormented by guilt after his wife's death and had hit the bottle hard. He'd drifted from place to place, finding jobs where he could and just as quickly losing them due to his perpetual drunkenness. He'd eventually ended up in Philadelphia where he'd died in 1908, penniless and with a bottle of cheap booze clutched in his hand. On hearing of his death, Cordelia had, according to her jailers, "lost the will to live." She died in prison on March 7, 1910, with the official cause of death given as "softening of the brain due to melancholia."

Dead Man's Hand

Like most western European countries, Spain has a low crime rate and an even lower rate of violent crime. Murder is rare and serial murder rarer still. But that is not to say that Spain is exempt from these monsters. Consider the case of José Antonio Rodríguez Vega, a depraved rapist and killer of 16 elderly women; or of Joan Vila Dilme, a notorious medical serial killer; or Francisco Garcia Escalero, who cannibalized several of his 11 victims. None of these monsters, however, was quite as wanton as Alfredo Galán Sotillo, the so-called "Playing Card Killer."

Born in Puertollano, in the central Spanish province of Ciudad Real, Galán grew up to be a wholly unremarkable child. A painfully introverted boy, Alfredo drew even further into his shell after his mother died when he was ten years old. Then, as he entered high school, he seemed to undergo a dramatic change of personality, becoming the class clown and, later, student president. Psychologists would later suggest that this apparent personality change was all an act, a desperate cry for attention by a boy who felt a deep sense of isolation from his peers.

There is also an element of attention-seeking in the career that Galán
decided on after graduating high school. Tall, lanky, and stoop-
shouldered, he seems poorly suited to the life of a soldier. Yet that was
exactly the career path he chose, enlisting in September 1998 and
volunteering for a parachute regiment. He eventually attained the rank
of corporal and participated in missions supporting the U.N. in Bosnia.
Stationed in Mostar, a city that saw major fighting between Serbs and
Croats, Galán experienced death and atrocities at first hand, including
the loss of several of his comrades. Yet his major complaint was that,
as a peacekeeper, he was never allowed to use the weapons he'd been
trained to fire. Worryingly, he confided in his fellow soldiers that he
wanted to know how it felt to kill someone. He also developed a near
obsession with firearms and managed to get his hands on a Soviet-
made Tokarev TT-33 handgun. When Galán returned to Spain in 2002,
the weapon was smuggled in with him.

You might think that Galán would have been grateful to have escaped
the front lines of the Bosnian conflict, where 24 of his countrymen had
been killed. But you'd be wrong. The parachute regiment was next
dispatched to Galicia, on Spain's Atlantic coast, to assist with a clean-
up operation after the oil tanker Prestige ran aground. This angered
Galán, who complained to his colleagues and superiors that he had
signed up to fight, not to act as a glorified janitor. In his frustration, he
started acting out, drinking heavily and getting into fights.

Galán's behavior became so extreme, in fact, that the military
authorities shipped him off to Gómez Ulloa Hospital in Madrid for
evaluation. There, doctors diagnosed him with anxiety and prescribed
medication. That only worsened the situation, since Galán routinely
mixed his pills with alcohol. During one of his drunken escapades, in

March 2002, he crashed a stolen car and ended up being discharged from the army on medical grounds. Shortly thereafter, he applied to the Spanish police but was turned down. He found work eventually as a security guard at Madrid's Adolfo Suárez Madrid–Barajas Airport. That at least allowed him to wear a uniform and gave him the modicum of authority that he so craved.

But in truth, Galán felt humiliated by his new station in life. A perfect storm was brewing. Here was a man trained in the art of war and equipped with an unlicensed firearm; here was a man desperate for attention and seething with rage at the perceived slights that society had doled out to him; here was a man whose inhibitions were lowered by prescription anti-depressants and alcohol. In the end, it wasn't a question of whether Alfredo Galán would lash out but rather a question of when.

Many serial killers commit their first murder unintentionally, as the result of a sexual or physical assault gone too far. Not so Alfredo Galán. He fully intended to kill someone on January 24, 2003, the day that he shot 50-year-old Juan Francisco Ledesma to death in front of his two-year-old son. Ledesma was forced to kneel and then executed by a shot to the back of the head with Galán's Tokarev pistol at point-blank range. Galán then departed the scene, leaving the little boy traumatized but otherwise unharmed.

On February 5, twelve days after the Ledesma murder, Galán struck again, this time gunning down 28-year-old airport cleaner Juan Carlos Martín Estacio as he waited for a bus after completing his shift in the early morning hours. Although nothing was taken from the victim, the police flagged the murder as a robbery gone wrong. There was, however, one detail which puzzled them. Close to the body, officers found a playing card ("the ace of cups" in a Spanish deck). This detail was soon leaked to the media and was widely reported with the papers suggesting that it was the "calling card" of a serial killer. Galán, of course, was following every detail of the story and, although he had not left the card there himself, he liked the idea. From now on, a card would be left at the site of each of his killings.

Later that same day, Galán drove to Bar Rojas, a tavern about a mile away from his apartment. Entering the premises, he drew his Tokarev and started firing randomly at staff and customers. Bar patron Alcalá de Henares was shot as she stood talking on her phone, the bullet entering her eye and killing her instantly. Galán then turned the weapon on 18-year-old Mikel Jiménez Sánchez, the son of the bar owner, who was working as a waiter. He too, died at the scene. The bar owner was also shot but survived her wounds. Galán then dropped a three of cups playing card at the scene and fled, leaving terrified patrons to call the police.

By now, ballistics had linked all of the murders to the same weapon, and the Madrid police knew that they were hunting a serial killer. They also had a description of the killer, courtesy of patrons who had survived the Bar Rojas massacre. Unfortunately, those descriptions (as is often the case when given by traumatized victims) were wide of the mark. They allowed Galán to remain at large.

Galán's lust for blood was far from sated. But for now, he was lying low, watching with interest as the police pursued another suspect who, like Galán, was ex-military and had served in Bosnia. That gave Galán the leeway to plan his next attack. On March 7, he emerged on a leafy suburban street and gunned down 27-year-old Santiago Eduardo Salas. Galán then turned the gun on Salas's companion, 29-year-old Anahid Castillo Ruperti, but the weapon jammed. He fled, dropping a three of cups at the scene. By the time emergency services arrived, Santiago Salas was dead.

This latest murder whipped the Spanish media into a frenzy of graphic rapportage. And the case of the "Playing Card Killer" was now attracting international headlines, placing even greater pressure on the authorities to catch the murderer. They responded by bringing in a team of federal homicide investigators to work alongside the Madrid police, but that proved to be little more than window-dressing. On March 18, the killer struck again.

His target this time was a Romanian couple, George and Diona Magda, who were accosted in a passageway of their apartment building in broad daylight. The terrified victims were forced to kneel. George was then shot in the back of the head while Magda was shot three times, the bullets partially deflected as she threw up her arm to protect herself. She died in the hospital two days later.

Thus far in the investigation, the police had withheld certain details (including a description of the killer) from the public. But the latest double murder forced their hand. The following morning, El Pais, El Mundo and every other newspaper, throughout the capital and beyond, carried a trio of identikit pictures. Not one of these even closely resembled Galán. Then there was the profile of the killer drawn up by a forensic psychologist. It got some details right – the fact that the killer might be a shift worker and might have some connection to the

Balkans – but missed others. Most notably, it made no mention of a possible military background.

All of this greatly irked Alfredo Galán. The core motive behind his killing spree was his desperate need for attention. If the police could not even get basic details right, then what was the point. On July 3, 2003, he decided to set them straight on a few issues. That was the day that an inebriated Galán walked into a police station in his hometown of Puertollano and told the startled desk sergeant that he was the "Playing Card Killer" and wanted to surrender. Amazingly, the officer ejected him from the station with a warning not to waste police time. It was only when Galán returned in a more sober state the following day that he was placed under arrest.

Once in custody, Galán made a boastful confession to his interrogators, calmly talking them through the details of his crimes and bragging about the fact that he had surrendered rather than being captured. At his subsequent trial, he pleaded guilty to six charges of murder. He was sentenced to 142 years in prison. It is highly unlikely that he will never be released.

Desperation

Gary Amaya

What drives a man to murder? Is it greed, anger, revenge? Are some
men just born with a lust for blood and a reckless disregard for human
life? In Gary Amaya's case, it was none of the above. Well, perhaps
Amaya was angry, but in his case, he probably felt that it was justified.
Once he'd been an independent trucker, with an honest streak that saw
him turn down jobs where the clients wanted him to take the backroads
in order to avoid weighing stations. He'd also been a gun nut, a coin
collector and a history buff with a particular interest in World War II
and in the Kennedy assassination. But then the economy had taken a
bad turn, trucking jobs had dried up, and with it Amaya's sole source
of income had disappeared. He'd been forced to sell off his coin
collection and his beloved guns, all at knockdown prices. By the fall of
2010, Amaya's house in Rankin, Illinois, had holes in the roof that he
couldn't afford to fix, his water had been cut off due to unpaid utility
bills, and he was reduced to using a plastic bucket as a toilet. They say
desperate times call for desperate measures and Gary Amaya was
about as desperate as it gets.

On the morning of Tuesday, October 5, 2010, construction company
employees Rolando Alonso, Joshua Garza, and Matthew Burton were
working on a house on Stoney Island Avenue in Beecher, Illinois,
when a man pulled up in a pickup. He asked the men whether the
house was for sale and then engaged them in some small talk before
getting into his truck and driving off. About 20 minutes later, however,
he was back, this time asking if he could help himself to some
plywood that was strewn around the site. He then continued talking to
45-year-old foreman Alonso, while Burton and Garza got back to
work. Moments later, the two 19-year-olds heard a shot and saw
Alonso crumble into the dirt. Then, before the younger men could
react, the gunman shifted his aim and fired at Garza, hitting him in the
eye. He then fired at Burton and missed, as the young man was already
running, sprinting across the road and into a nearby cornfield where he
hid among the tall stalks, took out his cellphone and dialed 911. He'd
barely made the connection when the phone died on him.

Burton would remain hidden in the field, fearful that the shooter was
still hunting him, for ten minutes, until he heard the sound of sirens
approaching. The 911 operator had been able to triangulate his
position from his cell phone signal.

Rolando Alonso and Joshua Garza were both still alive, although in
critical condition. As the men were rushed to a local hospital,
detectives started questioning Matthew Burton about the shootings.
Burton said that the shooter was a tall, somewhat overweight, man
with a stubble of beard on his chin. He'd been wearing a green
windbreaker and a black beanie from which dark hair protruded. His
vehicle, according to Burton, was a white, late-90s model Ford pickup
with Illinois plates. A description of the shooter and his vehicle were
immediately circulated, with officers warned that the suspect was
armed and dangerous.

About an hour after the shooting at the construction site, 64-year-old Keith Dahl was driving near his farm in Lowell, Indiana, just across the state line from Illinois. Dahl had just pulled to the side of the road to check on his bean crops when another vehicle pulled up beside him and a burly man got out. The stranger engaged Dahl in conversation, asking about the possibility of keeping honeybees in the area. Dahl replied that he might be interested in starting such a venture on his property, and the stranger then produced a pen and a scrap of paper on which he jotted down his name and phone number. This he handed to Dahl through the open window.

But the farmer had just accepted the paper when the stranger pulled a gun and started firing, pulling off three shots in rapid succession. Badly wounded but not killed, Dahl had the presence of mind to lie still, pretending to be dead. He could feel the man going through his pockets, removing his wallet. Then the shooter fired again, hitting Dahl in the side before walking to his truck, getting in and driving away. Dahl waited just a few minutes more before starting up his own vehicle. Wincing in pain and losing blood at an alarming rate, he nonetheless managed to drive to his house from which he called 911. He was taken to Crown Point Hospital where, despite the four bullets wounds he'd suffered, doctors were able to stabilize his condition. Keith Dahl had had a very lucky escape.

Over in Will County, Illinois, Rolando Alonso had not been so fortune. The 45-year-old father of nine succumbed to his wounds at 2:55 p.m. that same afternoon, even as Keith Dahl was being rushed to hospital. The other victim, Joshua Garza, would also survive, although with horrible injuries. In any case, with one dead, this was now a murder inquiry, one that had already been linked by the jurisdictions involved.

Deputies in Will County, Illinois, and Lake County, Indiana, knew that they were hunting the same man, a burly and somewhat unkempt individual, standing at around 6 feet and weighing between 220 and 260 pounds. There was some confusion, though, about the vehicle he was driving. Matthew Burton had described it as a white, late 90's Ford; Keith Dahl said it was a light blue Chevy Cheyenne of late 80's/early 90's vintage.

On the afternoon of October 5, some six hours after the shooting of Keith Dahl, officers in Schererville, Indiana, pulled over a light blue Chevy truck and questioned the driver, a man named Brian Dorian. Dorian was, in fact, a police officer from Lynnwood, Illinois, although he was currently on disability leave after injuring his shoulder on duty. After answering some routine questions, he was allowed to leave.

But this would not be the last time that Dorian featured in the investigation. On October 7, the Indiana State Police issued an improved sketch of the suspect, now dubbed the 'Honeybee Killer' because of the questions he'd asked Keith Dahl before opening fire on him. When Schererville officers got a look at the upgraded sketch, they were immediately reminded of the man they'd pulled over a few days earlier, Brian Dorian.

In fact, while the sketch did bear some resemblance to Dorian, there were several key differences between him and the 'Honeybee Killer.' Dorian was younger and fitter, not so stoutly built. He wore his hair in a crewcut whereas the killer had been described as having locks of hair protruding from his beanie. Nonetheless, Dorian was placed under surveillance. Then Matthew Burton was shown a photo array and immediately picked out Dorian as the man who had shot his co-workers.

In the early morning hours of October 8, 2010, detectives, backed up by a SWAT team, carried out a raid on Brian Dorian's residence. Dorian was arrested and despite vehemently proclaiming his innocence, he was charged with murder. His alibi, that he'd been at home working on his computer at the time of the shootings, seemed flimsy at best. When Matt Burton picked him out of a police lineup, the police were certain that they had their man.

But that optimism lasted only until investigators got a call from another of the surviving victims. Keith Dahl was recovering at home when he saw a news item on Brian Dorian's arrest. He immediately called the police and told them that they had the wrong man. There was only one way to clear up the discrepancy. Dorian's computer was handed over to forensic experts who were asked to refute or confirm his alibi. The answer was probably not what the Honeybee Killer task team wanted to hear. Dorian had indeed been working on his computer at the time of the shootings. He was not the killer.

Brian Dorian was released from police custody on October 15 with all charges against him dropped. The police now began working the only viable clue they still had, trying to trace the blue Chevy Cheyenne. That, however, would prove a nigh on impossible task. By December 2010, the case had ground to a shuddering halt. The Honeybee Killer, meanwhile, appeared to have gone into hibernation.

On the afternoon of Saturday, December 11, 19-year-old Karen Groder
was working a shift at the L.A. Tanning Salon in Orland Park, Illinois.
It had been a relatively quiet day when, just after 6 p.m., the door
swung open and a heavyset man entered. He approached the counter
and engaged Karen in conversation, asking about prices for tanning
treatments. Then, suddenly, he produced a gun, pointed it at the
startled receptionist, and demanded money. Karen had barely had an
opportunity to respond when he rounded the counter and passed a
length of rope to her. He told her to tie her hands, then checked the
bonds before tying her to the chair. It was at that moment that another
customer entered the store.

Jason McDaniel immediately realized that something was wrong when
he heard the receptionist crying. Then he, too, found himself facing the
armed gunman, handed a piece of rope and told to tie his own hands.
McDaniel tried to reason with the man, telling him that he was
carrying a large amount of cash which the man could have if he let
them go. The man told him to shut up and do what he was told.
McDaniel then told him that he had a 16-month-old daughter at home.
The gunman said he didn't care. What really worried McDaniel was
that the man wasn't masked. Was he really going to let them live if
they could identify him? Probably not. McDaniel resolved there and
then that he was going to have to wrestle the gun from the man... if he
got the chance to make a move without being shot, that is.

Fortunately, the gunman made it easy for McDaniel when he placed
his gun on the counter and bent down to pick up a length of rope from
the floor. Seizing his chance, McDaniel charged him. The gunman was
bigger, but McDaniel was younger and fitter. As they fought for
control of the weapon, a shot went off, hitting the gunman who
collapsed to the floor. Now McDaniel had the gun and was holding it
on him. In the meanwhile, Karen had worked her hands free and rolled

her chair over to the counter where she dialed 911. The police were on the scene within minutes.

The would-be robber was rushed to Advocate Christ Medical Center where ER staff made a valiant but ultimately unsuccessful attempt to save his life. Within an hour, he was dead. In the meantime, officers working the crime scene had found a light blue Chevy Cheyenne parked outside the tanning salon. A quick check returned that it was registered to Gary Lee Amaya of Rankin, Illinois. The other key piece of evidence was the .38 snub-nosed revolver that Jason McDaniel had wrestled away from Amaya. Ballistics would soon link it to the murder of Rolando Alonso and the shootings of Joshua Garza and Keith Dahl. The Honeybee Killer had been caught at last.

In the aftermath of the Honeybee Killer case, there was much speculation about what had driven Gary Amaya to murder. Amaya's father believed that his son was suffering from mental illness, made worse by his mother's recent death from cancer. Friends and associates of Amaya offered a different assessment. They recalled that Amaya as a quiet, gentle man with a good sense of humor. They reckoned that he'd been driven to kill by his hopeless situation. Desperation drives men to desperate deeds.

Kiss the Girls and Make Them Die

Minander Kohli

Hannah Foster was a bright girl. The pretty 17-year-old was a straight-A student and planned to attend university after high school to study medicine. But all of those dreams came to an abrupt end on the night March 14, 2003, when Hannah was returning home from a night out with friends in Southampton, England. She was less than a half-mile from home when she was spotted by a man, a sexual predator who decided on the spur of the moment that he had to have her.

Maninder Pal Singh Kohli was an Indian national who had come to the U.K. in 1993 for an arranged marriage. That union had produced two children in the interceding ten years, but it was far from happy. Maninder and his wife were often involved in shouting matches that sometimes necessitated the intervention of the police. The cause of those arguments often related to the couple's finances. Maninder was addicted to gambling, and much of the paltry salary he earned as a sandwich delivery driver went on that obsession. Not only that, but he had run up debts of over £16,000 to fund his habit.

Aside from gambling, Maninder Kohli had at least two other vices. One was an unhealthy fixation with teenaged girls, particularly pale-skinned English blondes; the other was a predilection for the bottle. When tempers flared at home, he often headed for the local pub where he would drink himself into a stupor. It was on one such night, just as he was staggering out of the pub, that he spotted Hannah Foster. He decided there and then that he was going to have sex with her.

Walking quickly from the bar, Kohli went to his delivery van and started tracking Hannah through the darkened streets. Along a particularly dark stretch of road, he saw his chance and suddenly did a U-turn and veered in front of Hannah, mounting the sidewalk and cutting her off. Before she'd even had a chance to react, Hannah was pulled into the van and ordered into the passenger seat. She was told to remain there and not to try anything, under threat of violence. Then her abductor started driving towards the outskirts of town, looking for a quiet spot where he could rape her.

While this was going on, Hannah made one final, desperate bid for help. She punched 999 into her phone, hoping the operator would pick up on what was happening. The operator who picked up the call could make out a conversation between a man with a strong Asian accent and a woman. The man was asking the woman's name, her age, where she lived. Unfortunately, because Hannah was too terrified to speak directly to the 999 operator, the call was terminated.

With it went Hannah Foster's last chance of survival. Kohli had now pulled his vehicle to a stop along a quiet country lane. There, he pulled his terrified victim from the van, ripped off her clothes and savagely raped her. According to his later confession, he then apologized for what he'd done, asked Hannah to forgive him and begged her not to tell anyone. He said that he was a married man with two young children and had never done anything like this before. But Hannah was adamant, she was going to tell her parents and they, in turn, would report the matter to the police. She knew from the branding on the van where Kohli worked, so he would soon be arrested. Kohli said that he panicked in that moment, grabbed Hannah from behind and strangled her. He then drove off, leaving the teenager's body lying by the roadside where it would be found two days later.

The murder, of course, received massive coverage in the British media. Kohli spent three anxious days, expecting the police to arrive on his doorstep at any moment. Eventually, his panic got the better of him. On March 17, he asked his father-in-law for a loan, saying that he had to return to India as his mother had fallen ill and was not expected to live much longer. The following day, he was on a flight out of London Heathrow, bound for India.

Kohli was met at Delhi airport by his younger brother Ishtpreet, a constable with the Indian police. They drove from there to the family home in Mohali, where Kohli would spend the next ten days. As those days passed with no news of the murder, he probably started to believe that he'd gotten away with it, that he could lie low in India for a while longer before returning to the U.K.

Unbeknownst to Kohli, the British police had already made significant progress in the case. They had obtained a DNA sample from Hannah's clothing and, although they didn't have a match on file, it could be tested against a suspect should they arrest one. There was also a tip-off, received after the case was featured on the BBC program,

Crimewatch. One of Kohli's work colleagues had suggested his name to police. When police then learned that Kohli had fled the country, they impounded his van. Hair and fiber evidence lifted from the vehicle suggested that Hannah had been inside it. The police also placed Kohli's van on the highway between Southampton and Portsmouth on the night Hannah went missing, using evidence from automatic license plate recognition software. Completing the picture was data from cell phone masts which put Kohli and Hannah in the same area.

Kohli was oblivious to all this, of course, convinced that he had escaped justice. But his hopes were dashed on March 27, when he received a long-distance call from his father-in-law saying that the police were looking for him in connection with Hannah's murder.

The British authorities had, in the interim, filed an application for his extradition. That paperwork would eventually be signed on April 3, but by then Kohli already had a six-day lead on his pursuers. He'd slipped away from his family home on March 28. Over the next seven months, there would be sightings reported from Bangalore, Delhi, Mysore, Chennai, and Dehradun.

It is uncertain whether Kohli ever was in any of those places. He was, however, in Darjeeling, West Bengal, arriving in February 2004 and taking up work at a Red Cross camp near Kalimpong. By now, he was using the alias Mike Dennis and posing as a doctor, administering hepatitis vaccinations to the camp's children. He had also caught the eye of Bharati Das, daughter of the camp administrator. After a whirlwind four-month romance, the couple married in June 2004, with

Bharati blissfully unaware of her husband's criminal past – or the fact that he already had a wife and children.

But the couple's wedded bliss would last only three weeks before Kohli's face was again adorning the front pages of the national newspapers, alongside a five-million-rupee reward put up by Hannah's parents for information regarding his whereabouts. The Fosters had, in fact, been actively involved in the investigation from the very start and had traveled to India on four occasions to appeal for help. It is largely through their efforts that the story remained in the news, even when the Indian police appeared to be dragging their heels in the hunt for Kohli.

Kohli had established a comfortable little life for himself in Kalimpong. Now he had to run again. His new wife was told that they had to cross the border into Nepal, although Kohli never explained why it was necessary, or indeed, so urgent. As it was, they never made it out of the country. Kohli was arrested at a bus stop in Panighatta, near the Nepalese border. That was on July 14, 2004, exactly 17 months from the day on which he had raped and murdered Hannah Foster.

Kohli was taken back to Chandigarh, where he took the unusual step of appearing on television to confess his crimes. The interview, however, was largely self-serving. He said that he'd been very drunk on the night he'd abducted Hannah and had only killed her because she had refused his pleas not to report the rape. He had fled because he had known that an Asian man who killed a white teenager would not get a fair trial in Britain. Kohli would later withdraw this confession saying that it had been coerced. Since it was given to a television journalist rather than the police, it is difficult to see how that is possible.

But at least Kohli was in custody, and it was only a matter of time and red tape before he was returned to Britain to answer for his horrific crimes. That date eventually came around three years later on July 28, 2007, when his flight touched down at Heathrow. Five-and-a-half months later, Kohli stood before Winchester Crown Court charged with murder, kidnapping, rape, and perverting the ends of justice.

Kohli entered not guilty pleas to each of the charges against him, offering a bizarre defense. He admitted to having sex with Hannah but said he had been forced into it by his work supervisor. He suggested that the supervisor had then strangled Hannah in order to frame him.

It was a quite ludicrous story, especially given the enormity of the evidence against Kohli, which now included a DNA match to the "biological material" found on Hannah's clothing. It was no surprise when the jury returned a guilty verdict.

On November, 25, 2008, 41-year-old Maninder Kohli, was sentenced to life in prison, with a recommended minimum term of 24 years. He will be 63 before he becomes eligible for parole.

Pretty Awful

At a few minutes before midnight on August 3, 1992, the 911 line
serving the small community of Peru, Indiana, jangled into life. On the
line was a woman named Susan Grund who calmly told the operator,
"It's my husband...There's blood on him." The operator then obtained
details and dispatched units to the address given by the caller. By then,
the word was already out and phone lines all across town were abuzz
with the news. Susan's husband, Jimmy Grund, was a prominent
citizen of the small Indiana town, a partner in the town's main law
firm, a former county prosecutor.

As police officers arrived at the Grunds' spacious country home, Susan
immediately offered the opinion that her husband had been shot after
surprising a burglar. She would continue to track the officers through
the house as they went about their business, chattering ceaselessly
about her burglary theory, as though she could convince them by force
of repetition.

But the crime scene evidence did not bear her out. Sure, a walk-in closet had been ransacked and jewelry apparently taken; sure, drawers had been pulled out and the contents of two suitcases spilled on the floor. To experienced investigators, it looked staged. In any case, the position of Jimmy Grund's body contradicted his wife's theory. Grund had been shot through the eye while sitting on a sofa in his bedroom. On the coffee table before him were bills, checks and other paperwork. It was as though he'd been shot while working. In other words, it was the burglar who had surprised him, rather than the other way around. Why then shoot him? Why not just flee as burglars are apt to do in such a situation?

The police didn't know the answers to those questions but they had a pretty good inkling. It all pointed to the newly-widowed Mrs. Grund.

Susan Grund was born in Peru, Indiana, in 1958. Her birth name was Sue Ann Sanders and she was one of seven children raised dirt poor on the wrong side of town. Her father was an abusive alcoholic who, if Susan is to be believed, physically and sexually abused her during her childhood. Nonetheless, she grew to be a slim and attractive girl with a dazzling smile and heaps of self-confidence. She also became sexually promiscuous during her teens, gaining the nickname One-Night Stand Sue Ann among the local boys.

At 17, Sue Anne quit school, rebranded herself as Susan and moved to the regional hub city of Kokomo, Indiana. There, she started dating a local musician named Ronnie Lovell, marrying him just a few weeks after they met. The couple later moved to Ronnie's hometown of Oklahoma City, where Ronnie worked construction during the day and did gigs at night. Susan, meanwhile, was managing the apartment complex they were living in. That gave her a lot of free time, and she put most of it into her favorite pursuit. Susan was addicted to sex and seldom turned down the opportunity to indulge. After sleeping with just about every man in the building, and a few more besides, she settled eventually on a regular lover, a rangy truck driver named Gary Campbell. When Ronnie found out and confronted her about it, she left him and moved into a trailer with Campbell.

In 1979, Susan fell pregnant with Campbell's child and divorced Ronnie Lovell. She and Campbell married soon after, and their son, Jacob, was born within months of the wedding. Now the second marriage followed the template of the first. Susan began sleeping around, cheating on her husband with any man who would have her. Her friends were always astonished by her sexual appetite. Susan would pick up a man in a bar and be in the back of his car having sex within minutes of their first hello. She just could not seem to get enough.

Given the way that they'd met, Gary Campbell must have known about his wife's sexual appetite. Nonetheless, he found that he could not stomach Susan's behavior and, within two years, the marriage was over. Barely out of her teens, Susan was already twice divorced. She did not remain so for long. Susan Campbell was about to make a step up in the world.

Tom Whited was a college-educated man, a former Army captain, a homeowner. He was also a recent widow, having recently lost his wife, Cheryl, to leukemia. Whited worked at Perry Filters, an Oklahoma City manufacturing firm owned by his late wife's father. When Susan also started working there, the sparks flew almost immediately

Lester Suenram, Tom Whited's former father-in-law, was less than
pleased with the relationship. Cheryl had only been dead six months
and, as Lester reminded Tom, Susan was a married woman. But Tom
wasn't listening. He'd fallen hard for Susan. In 1982, after Susan
obtained a divorce from Gary Campbell, Tom Whited proposed and
Susan said yes. They were married in the fall and thereafter settled
down to life in Whited's luxury home on Lake Hefner. The house had
been a wedding gift to Tom and Cheryl from Cheryl's father.

Susan and Tom had started life with an instant family. Susan's son
Jacob was now three years old, the same age as Tom's son, Tommy.
The two were just months apart, and Susan often told people that they
were twins. Tommy was soon addressing his new stepmother as
"Mom."

From the outside, it looked like the Whiteds were all just one big,
happy family. But that impression was deceiving. A few months after
Susan married Tom Whited, Tommy was admitted to an Oklahoma
City hospital with a fractured skull and brain swelling. Susan tearfully
explained to the doctor that Tommy had fallen and struck his head.
However, Tommy gave a different account. "My mommy hit me," he
said tearfully. Unfortunately, hospital staff failed to report this to the
police. Their lenience would have dire consequences.

Over the months that followed, Tommy was often seen sporting cuts
and bruises. His behavior also changed. The once happy little boy was
transformed into a nervous wreck who always seemed to be cowering
for fear of a beating. And yet there was no help for him, least of all

from his love-struck father. In Tom Whited's eyes, Susan could do no wrong.

In May 1983, Tommy was again admitted to the hospital, this time unconscious and suffering from a brain hemorrhage. Susan claimed that he had tripped over the family dog and hit his head on the sidewalk but this time the doctor wasn't buying it. The child had quite obviously been subjected to sustained abuse, with bruises on his head, torso and limbs. There were also multiple cigarette burns, while damage to his rectum indicated sexual assault. It would later be determined that the little boy had suffered permanent brain damage.

The police were called and Susan was arrested and charged with felony child abuse. Under interrogation, she stuck to her absurd story, that all of Tommy's injuries were caused by the boy's own "clumsiness." No one but her husband believed her. Lester Suenram, meanwhile, was outraged at the harm caused to his grandson. He launched a campaign to ensure that Susan would be prosecuted to the full extent of the law. Unfortunately, it was not to be. Susan was allowed to plead guilty to a single felony count of child abuse. For the crime of beating her stepson into a near vegetative state, she was given a ludicrously lenient five-year suspended sentence.

There were, however, other repercussions. Tommy Whited was removed from his father's care, with custody passing to his grandfather, who at least had the financial means to pay for the boy's ongoing medical care. Susan also lost custody of Jacob, who was sent to live with his father, Gary Campbell. As for Susan's marriage, the trauma appears to have done nothing to dull Tom Whited's passion for her. He continued to stick by the woman who had beaten his young son nearly to death. It was only after Susan fell into her old habit of sleeping around that he eventually walked out on her. He would later describe her as "the world's greatest liar."

In the summer of 1984, Susan was pregnant with Tom Whited's child and at a loose end following the breakdown of her third marriage. She decided to head back to her hometown, where she was soon working the local bars, picking up men for casual sex. Even in maternity clothes, she was still an attractive woman. It was through the Peru bar scene that she met a couple of cops who decided to play a practical joke on a friend of theirs. They set up a blind date for him with Susan, telling him that she was a real looker but failing to mention that she was pregnant.

That friend was Jimmy Grund, and the practical joke backfired badly. Almost from the moment Jimmy laid eyes on Susan, he was entranced. Here was this gorgeous woman, 14 years his junior, who appeared to be interested in him. It is easy to see how he might have fallen. As for Susan, Jimmy may have been slightly balding and carrying a bit of extra weight, but he was rich and he was available. She had a child on the way. She was going to need support.

A few months after they met, Jimmy waited anxiously at the hospital while Susan gave birth to her daughter, Tanelle. Days later, the couple and newborn traveled to Florida, where Jimmy and Susan were married on December 6.

In the early months of the marriage, Susan decided that she wanted to regain custody of her son, Jacob, who was still living with Gary

Campbell in Oklahoma City. Having a lawyer for a husband was, of course, a useful tool in this endeavor, but it came with a wrinkle. Susan had to admit to Jimmy that she had a criminal conviction for child abuse. She couched it in the most favorable terms, tearfully professing that the child had suffered an accident and that she had been made a scapegoat by an overzealous prosecutor.

With his background as a prosecutor, Grund could easily have checked the facts for himself. Had he done so, he would quickly have learned that Susan was lying. But, like Tom Whited before him, Jimmy refused to believe anything negative about his wife. Instead, he contacted Gary Campbell directly and lured him to Indiana with financial inducements and the promise of a job. He then persuaded Campbell to allow Susan to act as caregiver for Jacob. Before Campbell left the area months later, he signed the legal paperwork, transferring guardianship of Jacob to Susan. Jimmy also convinced Tom Whited to sign over permanent custody of his daughter, Tanelle.

Susan appeared to have hit the jackpot in marrying Jimmy Grund. In the summer of 1986, Jimmy spent $175,000 on the construction of a contemporary-style home in woodland on the edge of town. In a financial depressed area of the country, this was considered an outrageous sum. At the same time, Jimmy set Susan up in business, bankrolling a downtown boutique, Clothes by Susan. The Grunds were among the elite of Peru society, such as it was. They frequently hosted cocktail parties or were guests at society events. For a girl from the wrong side of the tracks, it must have been a heady experience. For a woman like Susan Grund, it wasn't enough.

Susan was soon the subject of town gossip over her sexual exploits. She was linked with a local accountant, a hunky cop, a Baptist minister, friends of her husband, deadbeats who she picked up from local bars. There were even rumors that she had seduced her stepson, David. To be fair, many of these stories might have been just small town gossip. But quite a few emanated from Susan herself. She seemed to take great pleasure in the power she was able to wield over men. She often shared the graphic details of these encounters with friends, with her sisters, even with her mother.

It seems impossible that Jimmy would not have heard the stories about his wife. In fact, his own mother once confronted him about Susan's reputation and asked what he planned on doing about it. Jimmy had simply shrugged. By the early nineties, the embers of the hot romance had gone decidedly cool. Jimmy was spending more and more time away, fishing with friends or drinking himself into a stupor. In the summer of 1992, he began talking to a lawyer about ending his marriage.

Susan was probably not aware at this time that her husband was planning to divorce her. It would, therefore, have come as a rude shock when Jimmy broke the news to her during a family vacation to Alaska in July 1992. He told her that he planned on filing the divorce papers as soon as they got home but, of course, he'd never get the chance. On Monday, August 3, 1992, Jimmy Grund was shot to death in his bedroom.

It is impossible to imagine how Susan thought she would get away with it. Just about everyone in town knew that the marriage was in trouble, that Jimmy had begun divorce proceedings, that Susan's philandering ways were about to catch up with her, that she was about to be left high and dry. How would she not be a suspect?

But suspecting Susan of murder and pinning Jimmy's murder on her were different things entirely. There was a decided lack of incriminating evidence. Most importantly, the police did not have a murder weapon. It would be left to Susan Grund, herself, to break the case. She never had been very good at keeping her mouth shut.

On September 2, a month after the murder, Susan confided in her sister and mother that she had shot Jimmy to death, using a gun that she had stolen from her stepson's home. Nellie Sanders and Darlene Worden were initially sympathetic to Susan's cause, even helping her hide the murder weapon by placing it in the bottom of a large copper pot and then filling the pot with concrete. But after keeping the deadly secret for two months, Darlene's conscience eventually got the better of her. She went to the police and told all. Within 36 hours, Susan had been arrested and charged with murder.

Susan Grund's murder trial got under way on September 27, 1993, with the defendant pleading "not guilty" and offering an alternate suspect. During her testimony, she tearfully informed the court that she had been involved in a sexual relationship with her stepson, David. She suggested that David might have murdered his father in a fit of jealousy over her affections.

It was a quite outrageous claim and one that was vigorously denied by David Grund on the witness stand. But Susan had achieved her objective. She'd created a reasonable doubt which proved impossible for some jurors to overcome. It resulted in a hung jury, leaving the judge no option but to declare a mistrial.

The second trial, in March 1994, was a much more straightforward affair. Susan's defense attorney convinced her that her revelations regarding the alleged affair with David would hurt her case and suggested that she not say anything about it. That proved to be a bad move. Without an alternate suspect to muddy the waters, the jurors quickly reached a unanimous guilty verdict.

Susan Grund was convicted of first-degree murder and sentenced to 60 years in prison. She becomes eligible for parole in 2025, when she will be 67 years old. Although Susan still professes her innocence, there are few who believe her. Fewer still, sympathize with her plight. She might have been a pretty woman, but Susan Grund was undoubtedly a pretty awful person.

Double Jeopardy

Brenda Sue Schaefer had been dating Mel Iganatow for two years when she decided to end the relationship. Mel was possessive, he was controlling, he was physically and emotionally abusive. Finally, in September 1988, Brenda called time. She told Mel that she was moving on with her life and arranged to meet him to give back all the jewelry that he had bought her. On September 24, she drove to his house in Louisville, Kentucky, to do just that. She was never seen alive again.

Mel Ignatow was, of course, the immediate suspect when Brenda's car was found abandoned the next day. The vehicle had been left on a street less than half a mile from the house she shared with her parents. Having found the vehicle, Brenda's father phoned Ignatow and asked him about Brenda's whereabouts. Ignatow seemed surprised by the question. He admitted that Brenda had visited him the previous evening but said that she had left his house at around 11, and that he hadn't seen her since. Brenda's father didn't believe him. As soon as he hung up the phone with Ignatow, he dialed the Jefferson County police and told them that his daughter was missing and that he suspected Ignatow of involvement.

The case was assigned to Detective Jim Wesley of the Violent Crimes unit who brought Ignatow in for questioning that same day. During that interrogation, Ignatow repeated essentially the story he'd given Brenda's father – that Brenda had left his house at 11 p.m. and that he hadn't seen her since. But Ignatow's demeanor was a dead giveaway to an experienced investigator like Wesley. He was cocky, overly friendly, almost challenging the detective to prove that he was lying. Wesley, of course, couldn't do that, not without evidence. And there was none. If Ignatow was indeed involved in Brenda's disappearance, he'd done a good job of covering his tracks.

Months passed with no clues as to what had become of Brenda Schaefer. The police were by now certain that she had been killed and remained convinced that Ignatow was involved. But they had nothing on him and Ignatow knew it. He appeared to be relishing his notoriety, never shying away from cameras or failing to give some smug soundbite to reporters.

Eventually, with no leads to work, the Louisville police called in renowned FBI profiler Roy Hazelwood and asked for his assessment of their main suspect. Hazelwood's report confirmed what they had felt all along. Ignatow was a narcissist, obsessed with his own self-image and with material possessions. He drove a Corvette, owned a 32-foot pleasure boat and lived in an affluent part of town. He was also known as a pathological liar, and Hazelwood believed that he showed characteristics of a sexual sadist, someone who gets off on the suffering of others. Hazelwood also noted that Ignatow appeared to regard the women in his life as possessions. He would not have accepted Brenda's intention to break up with him and may well have decided to punish her for it. And, having decided to kill her, he would have wanted to make the murder an enjoyable experience for himself. Brenda may well have been subjected to sexual torture before she was killed.

The profile made fascinating reading, but it did not amount to evidence. There was, however, one clue in the document as to how the police might proceed. U.S. Attorney Scott Cox thought that Ignatow's narcissistic need for publicity might be used against him. He asked Ignatow if he would be prepared to testify before a Federal Grand Jury to clear his name once and for all. Ignatow, of course, jumped at the opportunity. There was no way he was going to miss out on this moment in the spotlight.

The police were hoping that Ignatow would slip up in his Grand Jury testimony and, while he didn't do that exactly, he did make one major mistake. He mentioned the name of his former girlfriend, Mary Ann Shore. Shore was then hauled in to testify, and she was not quite as sharp as Ignatow. Asked whether she had ever met Brenda Schaefer, Shore said that she had … once. She was then asked to describe what Brenda looked like. "You mean the last time I saw her?" Shore responded. Then, realizing her mistake, she got up and fled the grand jury room.

The police now had a weak point to probe at. They brought Mary Ann Shore in for questioning and leaned on her. Before long, she had cracked, admitting that she had been present while Ignatow was torturing Brenda. The murder, she said, had happened at the Louisville home she had been renting. Ignatow had made elaborate preparations, carrying out "scream tests" to try and determine whether the neighbors would be able to hear any cries for help and also digging a deep hole in the woods behind the property to serve as a makeshift grave.

Brenda had been lured to Shore's home after returning the jewelry to Ignatow. There she was overpowered at gunpoint, tied up and subjected to hours of sexual torture during which she was raped, sodomized and beaten. Shore admitted that she was present during this ordeal and even confessed to taking pictures of Brenda being assaulted. However, she was adamant that she had not witnessed the murder. According to her, Ignatow had brought a bottle of chloroform with him and had later told her that he'd held a chloroform-soaked rag over Brenda's mouth and nose until she stopped breathing.

Shore insisted that she had not participated in the actual killing. Nonetheless, she was an accessory at best and might even find herself charged as a murder co-accused. She could be looking at life in prison or possibly even the death penalty. Faced with these potential outcomes, Shore begged prosecutors for a deal. They agreed, offering to drop all charges except that of tampering with evidence. In exchange, she would testify against Ignatow at trial and would also wear a wire in an attempt to get an admission to murder out of him.

On January 10, 1989, Mary Ann Shore led police to Brenda Schaefer's body, buried in the woods behind Shore's house. Brenda was lifted from the ground 16 months after she had disappeared. Shortly thereafter, Mel Ignatow was arrested and charged with her murder. It would be two years before he was brought to trial in Covington, Kentucky.

But the case against Ignatow was far from solid. The advanced decomposition of Brenda's body had made it impossible to retrieve any physical evidence. The prosecution could not even say with certainty how she had died. The case therefore rested heavily on Mary Ann Shore and, unfortunately, she turned out to be a terrible witness.

Weighing in at over 200 pounds, Mary Ann arrived in court wearing a mini-skirt which hiked high up her thighs when she sat down in the witness box. She appeared to regard the proceedings as a source of amusement, joking and giggling her way through her testimony. Then, under cross-examination, she was visibly flustered when the defense attorney suggested that it was she who had killed Brenda Sue Schaefer in a jealous rage over the affections of Mel Ignatow. All-in-all, Shore was a hindrance to the prosecution case rather than a help.

But prosecutors had one more trump card – a tape recording of a conversation between Mary Ann Shore and Mel Ignatow. This was played to the jurors and, although Ignatow never mentioned outright the act of murder, he did make certain incriminating statements. Unfortunately, one crucial word was obscured by static. The prosecutor insisted that Ignatow had said the word "site," in reference to the place Brenda was buried. But the jury heard it differently. They were sure he'd said "safe" and interpreted this as a reference to a buried strongbox, perhaps containing valuables. That discrepancy was enough for them to find Mel Ignatow "not guilty."

Ignatow's acquittal meant that only one person would be going to jail for the murder of Brenda Schaefer. Mary Ann Shore pled guilty to a charge of evidence tampering and served three years behind bars. Ignatow, meanwhile, was a free man, and the legal principle of double

jeopardy meant that he could never be tried again for Brenda
Schaefer's murder. Everyone knew that he had done it, but Ignatow
didn't care. In the eyes of the law, he was an innocent man.

Fate, however, was about to deal Ignatow the hand he deserved. Six
months after the murder trial, the new owners of Ignatow's former
home were doing some remodeling. While ripping up carpeting, a
workman came across a Ziploc bag containing several items of
jewelry. The man decided to report the find to the police, and the items
turned out to be those Brenda had returned to Ignatow on the night she
went missing.

This fortuitous find brought the police back to the house to carry out
another search. They had already gone through the property twice and
found nothing. This time, however, they hit the mother lode. Hidden in
a heating duct was a stack of quite horrific photographs. They showed
Brenda Schaefer being raped and tortured. The assailant's face was not
shown in any of the pictures, but Ignatow was easily identified by
distinctive moles on his body.

How the prosecution could have done with this evidence six months
earlier. Now, of course, it was too late. Even with such conclusive
evidence of wrongdoing, Ignatow could not be retried – at least not for
murder. He could, however, be prosecuted for perjuring himself in his
grand jury testimony.

Faced with the prospect of jail time related to those charges, Ignatow
tried to strike a deal with prosecutors. After years of denying
involvement in Brenda's death, he now admitted that he had sexually

tortured and murdered her. He even had the temerity to assure her
family that she had not suffered and had "died peacefully."

Convicted of perjury, Ignatow would spend five years in prison. But
the law wasn't done with him yet. There was another perjury charge to
answer. Shortly after Brenda's disappearance, Ignatow had become
involved in an altercation with her employer who had threatened to kill
him unless he revealed her whereabouts. Ignatow had filed charges
and the matter had ended up in court. During the course of that trial,
Ignatow had again lied under oath, and now he would pay the price. A
second perjury conviction landed him back in prison for another nine
years.

Ignatow was released from his second prison term in December 2006.
He emerged a broke and broken man who was often heard by his
upstairs neighbor shouting for God to put him out of his suffering.
That wish was granted to him on September 1, 2008, when he was
found dead at his home. It appeared that Ignatow had stumbled and
fallen, crashing through a glass coffee table and suffering lacerations
to his arm. He'd then stumbled towards the kitchen, probably in an
attempt to get to his phone and call 911. He never made it, collapsing
through blood loss and bleeding out on the kitchen floor.

A Message in Blood

Omar Raddad

On the night of June 24, 1991, police in the affluent village of
Mougins, on the French Riviera, received a call from a woman named
Colette Koster. Mme. Koster said that she was worried about her
friend and neighbor, Ghislaine Marchal. The wealthy 65-year-old
widow had been due to join Mme. Koster and her husband for lunch
on the previous afternoon but had failed to show. All attempts to reach
her since then had gone unanswered.

A detachment of gendarmes was duly dispatched to Mme. Marchal's
villa, entering the property through an unlocked side door. A search of
the living quarters turned up nothing untoward, and the officers then
proceeded to the basement where they found the door to the boiler
room closed and apparently barricaded from within. It took two beefy
gendarmes to shift the obstruction, and the officers then entered and
solved the mystery of Mme. Marchal's disappearance. The widow lay
on the rough floor, her body covered in blood. A bloodstained length
of wood lying nearby suggested that she had been beaten over the
head, but it was evident that she'd also been stabbed. Then one of the
officers noticed something that stunned him and his colleagues.

Written in blood on the inside of the door was the incriminating message: Omar m'a tuer (Omar killed me).

It did not take investigators long to find out who Omar was. He was 28-year-old Omar Raddad, a local gardener who worked part-time for Mrs. Marchal. Raddad was quickly tracked down and placed under arrest. Although he vehemently denied any involvement in Mme. Marchal's death, he was charged with murder. After all, the victim herself had pointed him out as her killer.

The savage murder of the 65-year-old widow sparked outrage across France, and with good reason. Mme. Marchal had not died easily. She'd been beaten into submission with the length of wood and then stabbed 18 times in the chest and abdomen. The medical examiner estimated that it would have taken her between 15 and 30 minutes to die. As for the time of death, that was easy to establish. Mme. Marchal had spoken to a friend on the telephone at 11:48 a.m. She been due at Mme. Kosters' home for lunch at 1 p.m. but had failed to arrive. Mme. Koster had phoned her at 1:30 p.m. but had received no reply.

Reconstructing a timeline of the crime, detectives believed that Mme. Marchal had been lured to the basement sometime during those missing two hours and attacked. Her killer had then left, believing her dead. But Mme. Marchal was not dead. She'd still possessed the strength to construct a barricade out of an iron bedstead and a metal bar to prevent her killer from re-entering the room. Then, realizing that she was probably going to die, she had scrawled her accusatory message in her own blood. She'd written the message twice in fact, once behind the door and once on a wall. The second message was incomplete and detectives believed that she had collapsed and died while writing it.

But here a few gaps emerged in the tidy theory. The first was a grammatical one. The French are sticklers for correct grammar, and the sentence "Omar m'a tuer" jangled with them. Mme. Marchal had mixed up her verb forms. The sentence meant literally: "Omar to kill me." Would an educated woman like Mme. Marchal, even in pain and shock and weak from loss of blood, have made such a basic error? Many observers thought not.

And then there was the second (incomplete) message, written low down on the wall opposite to the door. To get there, Mme. Marchal would have had to drag herself across the floor. Why then was there no blood trail?

These inconsistencies should have given the investigators pause. So, too, should the fact that they did not find a single print belonging to Omar Raddad in the basement. Would the uneducated gardener really have had the foresight to wear gloves or to wipe his prints away after the murder? Yes, in the opinion of the police who were also suspicious of a sudden change in Raddad's schedule. Usually, Raddad worked for Mme. Marchal on Sundays, but on the day of the murder, he'd worked for another customer instead, Mme. Pascal. Investigators believed he'd done so to distance himself from the crime scene. They were equally unimpressed by Raddad's alibi. According to his family, he'd been home, taking his lunch break, at the time the murder occurred. The police all but accused them of lying.

As the *Affaire Omar* headed for its date before the courts, French society was divided as to Omar Raddad's guilt or innocence. There were those who believed that Raddad, a Moroccan, was a victim of racial prejudice and there were those who believed that he was a heartless killer who should feel the full weight of the law. Unsurprisingly, those divisions typically ran along class and race lines.

Eventually, after two-and-a-half years in detention, Raddad was brought to trial in January 1994. As befits such a high-profile case, the legal representation on both sides was stellar. Appearing for the prosecution was Georges Kiejman, a former government minister and also the personal attorney of French President Mitterrand. Defending Omar was Jacques Vergès, whose client list included international terrorist Carlos the Jackal and Nazi war criminal Klaus Barbie.

According to the prosecution, Raddad had killed Mme. Marchal after she'd refused to give him an advance on his salary. Raddad, they insisted, was a slacker with a gambling addiction and an appetite for prostitutes. They provided no evidence to back up these claims. The defense countered by presenting a totally different picture of Raddad, introducing witnesses (including some of his employers) who described him as a diligent worker who was polite and easy going. They also pointed out that Raddad had no criminal record and had always had a good relationship with Mme. Marchal.

Then there was the issue of physical evidence with the prosecution leaning heavily on the message in blood. Two handwriting experts swore that the crude message was in Mme. Marchal's writing (the credentials of these so-called experts would later be heavily criticized). The defense, while presenting no expert of its own, raised doubts about the conclusions of these "experts." Vergès also wanted to know why the police had found no bloodstained clothing belonging to Omar Raddad. "Surely, after such a frenzied attack, he'd have been covered in blood," he said.

Vergès's contention was that the message in blood had been written by someone other than Mme. Marchal. Raddad could not have written it, even as an attempt at a double bluff, since he was illiterate. That meant that there had been someone else in the basement, and that person had likely killed Mme. Marchal and then written the message in an attempt to frame Raddad. "The ungrammatical nature of the accusation more or less proves it," Vergès said.

But not to the jury apparently. They found Omar Raddad guilty of murder and the judge then sentenced him to 18 years in prison. When a petition to the Supreme Court for a new trial failed, it appeared that Omar would spend the best part of two decades behind bars for a crime he still claimed he did not commit.

But then, in 1998, came a state visit to Morocco by French President Jacques Chirac. Chirac would not have expected the *Affaire Omar* to be on the agenda, but King Hassan had taken a personal interest in the case and asked Chirac to intercede on Raddad's behalf. Chirac did just that on his return to France, granting Omar a presidential pardon. After seven years behind bars (including his time awaiting trial), Omar Raddad was a free man.

But he was still a convicted murderer in the eyes of the law since the pardon did not absolve him of responsibility for the murder. That

simply was not enough for Raddad. Determined to have his name
cleared, he applied in January 1999 to have the conviction quashed.

This move came at considerable risk to Raddad. Under French law, he
could not be tried for the murder again – unless he initiated a new trial
himself. By applying to have his conviction set aside, he was doing
just that. If it went against him, he might well find himself back behind
bars.

But, on the face of it, Raddad had a strong case. Jacques Vergès was
still acting as his attorney, and this time he had brought in his own
(properly certified) graphologists who were prepared to swear that
Mme. Marchal was not the person who had scrawled the controversial
message on the wall. Even more importantly, Vergès had the backing
of DNA experts who had found traces of DNA from two other donors
mixed in with Mme. Marchal's blood. Neither of those donors was
Omar Raddad.

That evidence alone should have been enough to clear Raddad.
Unfortunately, Vergès decided to muddy the waters by introducing a
whole raft of unsubstantiated claims, claims which could best be
described as conspiracy theories. He suggested, for example, that there
had been a notorious criminal named Omar active in the area of
Mougins at the time of the murder. He suggested also that Mme.
Marchal's housekeeper was an unstable character who might have
been responsible for her death. Not content to stop there, he added the
murdered woman's family to the mix, saying that they'd been involved
in a bitter feud. He hinted that they might have hired a hitman to kill
her and frame Omar in order to get their hands on her money.

These unfounded accusations did Omar Raddad's case no good. In the end, the judges decided that there were insufficient grounds to reverse the original court decision. Omar was free but he was still, in the eyes of the law, a killer.

More than two decades after his original conviction, Omar Raddad continues the fight to have his murder conviction quashed. The problem is that he can only launch a new appeal if he has new evidence to present. That would now exclude the DNA evidence presented at his first appeal.

Blood Brothers

Serial killer brothers are a rare but not unheard of phenomenon in the United States. Perhaps the most infamous cases are those of the Brileys and the Lewingdons, responsible for 12 and 10 deaths respectively. But in each of those instances, the siblings in question worked as a team, doubling up on their helpless victims. What makes Danny and Larry Ranes unique is that they killed independently of one another, each of them following a path of destruction that terminated in the same place, a six-by-eight-foot cell.

Let's start with the case of younger brother, Larry. At around 5 p.m. on the afternoon of Saturday, May 30, 1964, a police officer from Kalamazoo, Michigan, was out on patrol when he spotted a Chevrolet sedan parked illegally at the roadside. He got out to inspect the vehicle and immediately noticed bloodstains on the rear bumper and papers scattered across the front seat. Since the vehicle's owner was nowhere to be seen, the officer made a call and arranged to have the Chevy towed to the impound lot. There, another officer popped the trunk and was stunned the find the blood-spattered body of a white male inside. Items found in the trunk identified the corpse as Gary Smock, a 30-

year-old junior high teacher from Plymouth, Michigan. His wife had
reported him missing that very morning.

The body was removed for autopsy, where it was discovered that
Smock had died of a gunshot wound from a .22 caliber weapon. The
bullet had entered the side of the head just below the ear and remained
lodged in the brain. A cord was tied around one wrist, suggesting that
the victim had been tied up before he was shot. The pathologist
estimated that he had died sometime between 6 a.m. and 2 p.m. on
Saturday. His watch and shoes were missing and his billfold was
empty, making it likely that the motive had been robbery.

Retracing the victim's last movements, detectives discovered that he
had traveled to Battle Creek, Michigan, on the Friday before he died
and had met with officials of the local Chamber of Commerce to
discuss plans for an upcoming Church of God youth convention in the
town. He had then driven to Allegan to visit his in-laws and had been
due home for dinner at six. However, he had phoned his wife, Thelma,
to say that he was running late. That was the last Thelma heard from
him. A sighting of Smock's car was reported at a Kalamazoo service
station around 11 that night, but that was the last time it was seen
before it attracted the attention of the police patrolman. Now, as a
forensic team examined the vehicle, they found a palm print and
fingerprint which did not belong to the victim or any of the family.
This clue, they hoped, would crack the case.

Before the investigators had a result on the prints, though, they
received word of another shooting, this one 60 miles away in Elkhart,
Indiana. Service station attendant Charles Snyder had been shot twice
in the head with a .22, and the killer had driven away with $100 from

the register. Was this case connected to the Smock shooting? Officers in Kalamazoo did a quick calculation. Smock's car had been filled up at 11:00 p.m. the previous night and now had half a tank of gas. That meant that it had traveled at least 100 miles in the intervening period. That put Elkhart within range. Ballistics did the rest. The same gun had killed both Smock and Snyder.

Police in Michigan and Indiana were now genuinely fearful. They had a killer on the loose, one who had committed two murders within a space of a few hours of each other and was very likely to kill again. Who knew where he would show up next?

But just as senior officers were discussing the formation of an inter-jurisdictional task force, there was an unexpected break in the case. A man named Arthur Booth phoned the police with an odd tale to tell. He said that an old buddy, 19-year-old Larry Lee Ranes, had showed up unexpectedly at his house on Thursday, June 4. Ranes appeared to have something on his mind, and he soon confessed it to Booth. He said that he had been hitchhiking across the country for the past three months and that he had "killed some people." Those deaths had been playing heavily on his mind, and so he intended to visit a priest the next day to make a confession. He was then going to shoot himself.

Ranes would never get to follow through on his suicide plan. He was arrested at Booth's home later that night. At the time of his arrest, he was wearing Gary Smock's stolen watch and shoes and carrying the handgun that had killed both Smock and Charles Snyder. Not that Ranes was denying the murders. He was in a confessional mood and readily admitted to killing the two men.

And those were not the only crimes he had committed. Ranes also confessed to gunning down Vernon LeBenne, a 20-year-old clerk who had worked at a service station just off the I-94, near Battle Creek; he said that he had shot and killed a man who had stopped to give him a ride in Death Valley, California; he confessed to shooting another gas station attendant, this one in Kentucky. Just 19 years old and Larry Ranes was already Kalamazoo's most notorious serial slayer.

And yet Larry wasn't even the most depraved killer in his family. That dubious honor would go to his brother Danny.

Danny Ranes was a year older than Larry, and the pair were said to be close, even though they frequently engaged in an aggressive form of sibling rivalry. "They both loved and hated each other," a family friend noted. And that assessment was borne out by Larry. "I used to hit Danny with boards, throw knives at him, shoot him with bows and arrows, shit like that," he said in a prison interview. "He'd do the same to me."

The source of this juvenile aggression, and of the men the Ranes brothers would later become, is not hard to find. Their father was an abusive alcoholic who beat his sons mercilessly, often, and without apparent provocation. By the time he walked out and abandoned the boys and their two sisters, they were deeply scarred emotionally. Larry talked frequently about suicide and had a brief stint in the military before embarking on his cross-country killing spree. Danny followed a similar path, although, compared to his brother, he was a late bloomer.

On the afternoon of March 3, 1972, 29-year-old Patricia Howk left her
home in Kalamazoo with her 17-month-old son, Cory. Howk was
bound for Topp's department store, but she had no idea that she was
being tracked by a predator. Danny Ranes, 28 years old and recently
paroled from prison on an assault charge, was on the hunt. After
spotting the attractive young mother, he decided to follow her. When
she parked her car on a quiet street, he pulled his van in behind her.
Then he waited.

An hour passed before Patricia returned, carrying some shopping bags
and with her son straddling her hip. Ranes waited until she had placed
the boy in the passenger seat of her car before he made his move,
approaching from behind, threatening Patricia with a knife and forcing
her into his van. There he tied her hands and then brutally raped her.

Patricia, no doubt afraid of what Ranes might do to her child, did not
resist. But when he put his hands on her throat and started squeezing,
she did fight back, putting up such a struggle that the van's door flew
open and the two of them tumbled out into the street. By now, Cory
had gotten out of the car and was standing on the sidewalk, crying.
Fearful of the attention this might attract, Ranes drew his knife and
stabbed the young woman repeatedly in the back until she eventually
lay still. Then he dragged the body behind a building, walked back to
his van and drove off, leaving the screaming toddler behind. The boy
would wander off and remain missing overnight until he was found the
next day, dehydrated and deeply traumatized.

The murder of Patricia Howk had not gone as Ranes had imagined it,
but it had left him with a taste for blood and a burning desire to do it
again. Soon he had acquired an accomplice, a 15-year-old miscreant

named Brent Koster who, despite his young age, was already 6-foot-6-inches tall. Koster was impressed by Ranes's boasts about the women he had abducted, raped and killed. When Ranes invited him along on his next "hunt," the teenager jumped at the opportunity. However, their early efforts did not go as planned; despite staking out malls and movie theaters for hours, they could not isolate a suitable victim.

Then, on the morning of July 5, a couple of victims fell into their laps. Ranes and Koster were at the Sprinkle Road service station (where Ranes worked) when Linda Clark and Claudia Bidstrup, both 19, pulled in to get gas. While they were filling up, Ranes popped the hood, saying that he was going to check the oil and water. Instead, he loosened some of the spark plugs. Then, when the girls couldn't get the car started, he suggested pushing it around to the back, so that he could take a look at it. There, Linda and Claudia were forced at knifepoint into Ranes's van, tied up and gagged. They were then subjected to an ordeal of rape by both men before being strangled to death. Later that evening, the bodies were loaded into their Opel and driven to a wooded area. The killers then poured gasoline over the corpses and threw a lit cigarette into the car. However, they left before the fire took hold and it soon burned itself out. The decomposed bodies would be found by some motorcyclists nearly two weeks later.

Right from the start, the police suspected that the double homicide might be connected to the murder of Patricia Howk. The knots used to tie the victims' hands were similar in each case and the women had been abducted from reasonably well-trafficked areas. That similarity in M.O. pointed to a serial killer, and the police were gravely concerned that the killer would soon strike again. They were right to be afraid.

On August 5, 18-year-old Patricia Fearnow was hitching rides near Kalamazoo and had the terrible misfortune of being picked up by Ranes and Koster. The Western Michigan University student was taken at knifepoint to a secluded area where she was repeatedly raped by both men over a period of six hours. They later drove her to Morrow Lake, a local beauty spot, where they gave her a glass of wine to drink while they each enjoyed a few beers and watched the sun set over the water. But if Patricia though that this indicated some sort of compassion in her attackers, she was mistaken. A short while later, she was dragged into the van and suffocated by having a plastic bag pulled tightly over her head.

The disappearance of Patricia Fearnow sparked a huge police investigation, with officers certain that she was the latest victim of the Kalamazoo killer. But the police had not been idle in the interim. They had been checking out businesses in the area that Linda Clark and Claudia Bidstrup had disappeared from and had questioned the owners of the Sprinkle Road service station. From them they'd learned that Danny Ranes had been on duty that day. Looking into Ranes background, detectives discovered that he was an ex-con who had served time for abducting a 17-year-old girl at gunpoint. That immediately made him a suspect. The police also learned about Ranes's lanky young friend, who could usually be found hanging around the station when Ranes was there.

Ranes and Koster were both brought in for questioning, and it wasn't long before Koster started talking. Striking a deal that would allow him to plead to one count of second-degree murder, Koster agreed to provide details of the Clark, Bidstrup, and Fearnow murders and to lead investigators to the spot where Patricia Fearnow's body had been dumped. He also agreed to tell what he knew about the Howk murder. Ranes had boasted to him about it often enough.

Unlike his younger brother, Danny Ranes did not appear to be in the least bit remorseful of the murders he had committed. Despite the damning evidence of his co-accused, Brent Koster, Ranes entered not guilty pleas to the four counts of first-degree murder brought against him. It did him no good. Found guilty on all counts, he was sentenced to life without parole. Koster, tried as an adult, was also given life, although the possibility of parole was not ruled out in his case.

And what of Larry Ranes? He, too, is serving a life term without parole. Larry has since legally changed his name, adopting the wordy moniker, Monk Steppenwolf (an apparent reference to Herman Hesse's acclaimed novel). With his beard and shoulder-length white hair, Larry even resembles a monk these days. But despite the name change and the change in appearance, the Ranes blood still flows in Larry's veins. Bad blood.

A House to Die For

Louisa Merrifield

Sarah Ann Ricketts was 79 years of age and lived alone in a modern bungalow in the seaside town of Blackpool, England. Mrs. Ricketts was known to be a lively old soul, with a liking for the odd nip of rum or brandy and an addiction to raspberry jam, which she ate by the spoonful. But her life had also been touched by tragedy, two husbands had died in the very bungalow where she now lived. Both had committed suicide by putting their heads in the gas oven.

Was it this that persuaded the independent Mrs. Ricketts to employ a housekeeper? Was it loneliness, a longing for human companionship? We shall never know for certain. What we do know is that, in early 1953, she placed an advertisement in the local newspaper for a live-in caretaker. One of those who applied was 46-year-old Louisa May Merrifield.

Like Mrs. Ricketts, Louisa Merrifield was twice widowed, although her husbands had died of natural causes. Currently, she was married to Albert Merrifield who, at 71, was 25 years her senior. Louisa had met

Albert while visiting her previous husband in the hospital and had tied
the knot with him shortly after she was widowed for a second time.
Those who met Albert said that he was odd and, quite possibly,
simple-minded.

Aside from her unusual marital situation, there were other things about
Louisa Merrifield that were off-kilter. One was that she had a criminal
record, having been convicted of ration book fraud. The other was that
she had held down 20 housekeeping jobs over the prior three years.
That statistic tells its own story, but Merrifield must nonetheless have
made a positive impression on Mrs. Ricketts because she hired her on
the spot.

And, at first, the Merrifields got on swimmingly with their new
employer. In fact, Mrs. Ricketts took such a shine to Louisa and Albert
that she changed her will, leaving her bungalow to them and, in the
process, disinheriting her only daughter. However, the relationship
soon soured. Before long, Mrs. Ricketts was complaining to the
drivers who delivered groceries to the address that she was barely fed
and that her employees were drinking her out of house and home.

In the meantime, Louisa May Merrifield was making a name in the
neighborhood as someone who was prone to making imprudent
comments. She once told a woman she'd only just met at a bus stop
that she'd caught her husband in bed with the old lady and that if it
happened again she'd "poison the old bitch and him as well." To a
friend, Veronica King, she boasted that she had inherited a £3,000
bungalow in Devonshire Road, Blackpool. When Mrs. King expressed
surprise and said she hadn't realized that Mrs. Ricketts had died,

Louisa quickly corrected her by saying, "Oh, she's not dead yet. But she soon will be."

On April 10, 1953, Mrs. Merrifield called her employer's regular physician, Dr. Yule, and asked him to certify that Mrs. Ricketts was "of sound mind." The reason for this odd request, she explained, was because she feared the old lady might soon die. Since Mrs. Ricketts had recently amended her will, she didn't want her relatives challenging it. Dr. Yule was happy to confirm that Mrs. Ricketts was quite sane. He also added that he did not expect her to die any time soon.

Just three days later, however, Merrifield was on the phone again, this time in a panic. According to her, Mrs. Ricketts was "at death's door" and she bade the doctor to come immediately. Since Dr. Yule was unavailable, it was his partner, Dr. Wood, who examined Mrs. Ricketts. Merrifield seemed almost annoyed when the doctor informed her that Mrs. Ricketts was suffering from a mild case of bronchitis and would be well soon.

That diagnosis, unfortunately, would prove to be inaccurate. The next morning, April 14, Dr. Wood was again called to the house and, this time, he found Mrs. Ricketts dead. Wood then called Dr. Yule, who would have to issue the death certificate. Yule, however, refused and insisted on a postmortem. That examination had not yet been carried out when the police began to get calls from friends and neighbors of Mrs. Ricketts, voicing suspicions about the possible involvement of Louisa and Albert Merrifield in Mrs. Ricketts's death.

Sarah Ann Ricketts had died just five days after Louisa Merrifield had expressed concerns about the validity of her will. That alone seemed suspicious, and the results of the autopsy would do nothing to allay the notion that Merrifield had something to do with her death. The pathologist found evidence of phosphorous poisoning, which he believed might have come from a commonly-used brand of rat poison called Rodine.

Finding evidence of poisoning and proving who had administered the poison were, however, two entirely different things. Both Albert and Louisa stoutly denied harming their employer, and searches of the residence and garden turned up no trace of Rodine. Neither was there any evidence that either Mrs. Ricketts or the Merrifields had ever bought the rat poison.

So were the police mistaken? Louisa Merrifield certainly did not act like a murder suspect. While the police were carrying out their search at the bungalow, she hired the local Salvation Army band to stand in the garden and play 'Abide with Me.' And when journalists started showing up to cover the story, she carried out trays of tea and cake to them. She seemed relaxed and jovial, they wrote in their papers. More than one writer admitted in his column that he liked her. The authorities, though, were of a different opinion. Despite having no evidence outside of local gossip, Alfred and Louisa Merrifield were arrested and charged with murder.

The trial of the Merrifields was held at Manchester Assizes and was a major media event, in Blackpool and beyond. Throughout it all, Louisa Merrifield maintained her jolly exterior, arriving each day in a taxi, smiling and waving to the gathered crowds. She appeared to be enjoying herself.

And why wouldn't she? After a lifetime of faceless drudgery, she was the center of attention, with camera flashes popping around her and newspaper headlines carrying her name. She also had every prospect of being acquitted. Other than a few ill-judged comments, what evidence did the prosecution have against her really? There was nothing that linked her to buying the Rodine, much less administering it to the old lady. In fact, even the cause of death was now being disputed. At least one distinguished expert stated on record that Mrs. Ricketts had not died of phosphorous poisoning but of liver failure brought on by old age and an eccentric diet.

Unfortunately for Louisa Merrifield, the people she most needed to impress, the jury, were not convinced of her innocence. All of those off-color remarks about Mrs. Ricketts' impending demise now came back to haunt Merrifield. So, too, did her tardiness in summoning a doctor to attend to Mrs. Ricketts. According to Merrifield's own testimony, the elderly woman had taken ill on the night of April 13, but she'd waited until the next morning to call Dr. Wood. And then there were Merrifield's actions after Mrs. Ricketts died. She immediately tried to arrange a cremation, stating that it had been the old woman's dying wish, something the Ricketts family disputed.

But the thing that arguably counted most against Merrifield was her light-hearted attitude to her employer's tragic death. All of those movie star entrances had made a poor impression on the jury. They found Louisa May Merrifield guilty of murder, while acquitting her

husband, who the judge had memorably labeled "a tragic simpleton."
The sentence of the court was death by hanging.

Louisa May Merrifield died on the gallows at Manchester's
Strangeways Prison on September 18, 1953. The executioner was
Albert Pierrepoint, who did not have far to travel in order to carry out
his grisly duty. He had been honeymooning in Blackpool and broke off
from his new bride for a few hours in order to perform the execution.

In the aftermath of his wife's death, Albert Merrifield returned to the
Devonshire Road bungalow which he now owned. He later gave up his
claim to the property in order to avoid a legal battle with the Ricketts
family. Albert would live for nine more years during which he was a
popular sideshow attraction in Blackpool, talking about the town's
most infamous murder.

Without Mercy

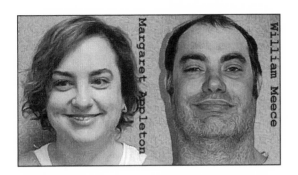

Joe Wellnitz was universally well-loved in the small town of
Columbia, Kentucky. The 50-year-old veterinarian lived just outside of
town in a farmhouse that he shared with his wife, Elizabeth, 40; and
Elizabeth's son and daughter from a previous marriage, Dennis, 20,
and Meg, 18. A love of animals, of course, went with his profession,
but Dr. Wellnitz went way beyond that. He genuinely cared for each
and every one of his four-legged patients, often shedding tears when
he lost one of them. And if their human minders couldn't afford his
fees, the good doctor would often waive them and treat the animal for
free.

Aside from his generosity and love of animals, Dr. Wellnitz was
known for one other thing, his unfailing reliability. So when
employees Derek Langwell and Cindy Litteral showed up for work on
the morning of Saturday, February 27, 1993, and found the clinic still
locked, they were immediately concerned. After waiting just a few
minutes, they decided to drive the short distance to the Wellnitz
residence.

Derek entered the house first and just as quickly came staggering out.
"Don't go in there," he warned Cindy as he set off in the direction of a
neighbor's house to call the police. Cindy, however, chose to ignore
the warning. She stepped into the hall and immediately saw what
Derek had seen, her employer lying on the floor in a pool of blood.
She could see right away that there was nothing to be done for Dr. Joe,
but Cindy knew that there were others in the house who might require
assistance. Bravely, she skirted the body, placed her hand on the
banister and started climbing the stairs. Any assistance she may have
rendered, though, was way too late. Elizabeth Wellnitz was in the main
bedroom, shot to death; Dennis was down the hall in his room, also
dead from a bullet wound; of Meg Wellnitz there was no trace.

The brutal triple murder was quite obviously beyond the capabilities of
the local cops in Columbia, and so jurisdiction fell to the Kentucky
State Police. Investigators were soon on the scene and quickly formed
a number of opinions about the crime. The first was that there had
been no forced entry to the property. This was odd since the
Wellnitzes were known to be security conscious and to always lock
doors and windows. The second was that the killer appeared to have
known the layout of the farmhouse. He appeared to have gone directly
to the bedrooms to kill his victims. Dr. Wellnitz had been killed
downstairs, but the investigators hypothesized that he'd come down to
fetch a pistol that he kept there. His intention was to defend his family,
but he'd been gunned down before he'd had a chance to do so.

Another conclusion drawn by the investigators was that the killer had
been a good shot. A total of ten bullets had been fired at the three
victims and only one had missed, embedding itself in a door frame.
But why? Why gun down an entire family, execution style, in the
middle of the night? It certainly didn't look like a robbery. Valuables
lay in plain sight and yet had been untouched. Then detectives noticed

an imprint on the carpet in one of the bedrooms and realized that something had been taken – a safe.

In the meantime, the mystery over the whereabouts of the fourth family member had been resolved. Meg Wellnitz was 100 miles away in Lexington where she was a student at Lexington Community College. It had been her good fortune that the murders had occurred on one of the weekends that she'd chosen not to come home.

Detectives were eager to interview Meg, but they walked into a roadblock when they encountered her boyfriend, Rhett Anson, a 25-year-old computer science grad student who seemed to regard himself as her protector and de facto lawyer. When the police did eventually get to talk to Meg, Anson was present, advising her which questions to answer and which to ignore. This attitude made him a suspect for a time, especially when it was learned that he owned a 9mm pistol and was considered a good shot. But Anson had an unshakable alibi and no real reason to harm his girlfriend's family. The same could be said for other suspects – a couple who rented a house on the Wellnitz property and Eric Wellnitz, Joseph's son from a prior marriage.

The murders, which had appeared imminently solvable at the beginning, were now beginning to look like they might end up in the cold case file. Word on the streets of Columbia was they were random shootings, committed by some drifter. But the police never believed that. The killings were too clinical, too planned. The prevailing thinking was that the killer had known the Wellnitzes and had probably harbored a grudge against them.

Of course, there was also the possibility of a financial motive. Joe Wellnitz had left behind a sizeable estate, valued at over $500,000. The surviving beneficiaries of that estate were Meg and Eric Wellnitz, both of whom had been miles away at the time of the murders, Meg in Lexington, Eric in Louisville. Not that that deterred the insurance company from reneging on settlement. Meg, they claimed, was a potential suspect in her father's murder and thus ineligible to profit from his death. In fact, the police had never flagged the teenager as a potential killer. And so, Meg lawyered up and forced the insurers to pay. She was probably none too happy about splitting the fortune with her half-brother, but $250,000 was still an awful lot of money to an 18-year-old.

The case, meanwhile, was dead in the water. All of the suspects had been interviewed, all clues followed up, all of the meager forensics processed. Yet the police had nothing. The Wellnitz crime scene was one of the cleanest the investigators had ever seen. In the words of one detective, it was as though someone had lifted off the roof of the house, dropped in three bodies and then put the roof back in place.

In late 2002, nearly a decade after the murders, officers of the Kentucky State Police again started looking at the Wellnitz murder files. Usually, in a cold case, it is DNA that provides the key evidence, but here there was none. All the detectives could do was to re-evaluate, re-interview, hope that something they'd missed in the past jumped out at them. Then, out of the blue, they received a tip from a woman named Regina Meade.

According to Meade, her ex-husband, father of her three children, was the killer of the Wellnitz family. His name was William Meece and he'd committed the murders, according to his ex-wife, at the behest of none other than Meg Wellnitz. It was a contract killing, Meade said, so that Meg could get her hands on her inheritance. And she could prove it. She had, in her house, the safe that had been stolen from the Wellnitz residence on the night of the murders.

Looking into William Meece's background, the police found even more reason to take the word of their informant. Meece was currently serving a 12-year jail term for conspiracy after he accepted a $2,000 payment to commit a contract killing. Moreover, he knew Meg Wellnitz. They had both been students at Lexington Community College at the time of the murders.

William Meece turned out to be a rather unstable character. Abandoned by both parents as a child, he had been raised by his grandparents, who had officially adopted him. When, he was 12 years old, Meece's grandmother had died and he'd been returned to the dubious care of his schizophrenic mother, Jan. Meece thought at this time that Jan was his sister, and she did nothing to discourage the notion. She also cut him off from society, withdrawing him from school and warning him against interacting with other people. As a result, he'd grown up a loner, quite possibly with mental and emotional problems. Jan would confess during her testimony at her son's trial that she often heard voices telling her to kill and that she was sure William heard the same voices, even if he wouldn't admit it.

The next step was to interview Meece and to hear what he had to say about the allegations against him. Detectives were expecting denials and protestations of innocence, but what they got instead was a deadpan confession to the killings. According to Meece, Meg Wellnitz had offered him a share of her inheritance in exchange for wiping out her family. She had also provided him with a key to the house and a sketch of the property's layout. That was how he had been able to enter the house and surprise the family in their sleep. It also explained how he had so efficiently carried out the killings.

Meece was arrested in his jail cell and charged with three counts of first-degree murder. At the same time, officers arrived at the home of Meg Wellnitz and took her into custody. The date was February 27, 2003, ten years to the day from the Saturday morning when Derek Langwell and Cindy Litteral had walked in on a bloodbath at the Wellnitz homestead. Meg had married and divorced in the intervening years and now went by her married name, Appleton. It was under that name that she was charged, under that name that she confessed and struck a deal, accepting a prison term of life with parole eligibility in 25 years.

William Meece might have struck a similar deal with prosecutors but had decided in the interim to take his chances with a jury and had recanted his confessions, saying that they had been coerced. That would prove to be a poor decision. Found guilty at trial, he was sentenced to death by lethal injection. He currently awaits execution at the Kentucky State Penitentiary in Eddyville.

Meg Appleton's jail sentence would also turn out to be a death sentence. She was found unresponsive in her cell on February 12, 2014, with her death ruled a suicide. The cold-blooded murder of her family had earned her ten comfortable, if guilt-ridden, years and another ten years locked up at the state penitentiary.

Marry Me and Die

In the modern vernacular, Emma LeDoux would be known as a "cougar," a woman who liked to party and who loved the company of men, the younger the better. Born Emma Head, in Jackson, California in 1871, LeDoux grew to be a pretty and precocious teen who walked down the aisle with her first husband when she was just 16. The marriage to Charles Barrett, however, was short-lived, with Emma obtaining a divorce. She then hooked up with a man named Bill Williams, moving with him to Arizona and marrying him there. Williams later died in suspicious circumstances, leaving his wife to claim a substantial insurance payout.

In September 1902, the now 31-year-old Emma Williams married for a third time, tying the knot with Albert N. McVicar in Bisbee, Arizona. And, as was to be expected given Emma's history, the marriage was soon in trouble, with McVicar departing for the Rawhide mine in Tuolumne County and his wife taking up residence in a California brothel. It was while working there that she met Eugene LeDoux, a punter who was soon infatuated with her and asked for her hand in marriage. Despite still being legally married to Albert McVicar, Emma

said yes and she and LeDoux were married. Thereafter, they moved
back to her hometown of Jackson.

Albert McVicar was, of course, oblivious to his wife's stint as a
prostitute and to her bigamous marriage. Despite the short and
tumultuous nature of their relationship, he still held a candle for Emma
and hoped that they might one day repair their marriage. In March
1906, he wrote to Emma and asked if she would meet with him in
Stockton, California, to talk things over. Emma agreed and on March
11 arrived at the arranged rendezvous, the California Hotel. There the
pair of them registered as "A.N. McVicar and wife."

The talk about a reconciliation quite obviously went well because, the
very next day, the couple visited Bruener's Store in Stockton and
ordered enough furniture to equip a small house. McVicar footed the
bill, but it was his wife who was calling the shots, arranging for the
items to be shipped to Jamestown.

The following day, "Mr. and Mrs. McVicar" departed for San
Francisco where they checked into the Lexington Hotel on Eddy
Street. That same evening, Albert McVicar took ill; a doctor was
called and diagnosed food poisoning. McVicar was on his feet within a
day after taking the medication prescribed for him. By then, Emma
had obtained some medication of her own. She'd cornered the doctor
and asked him for a prescription of morphine, to which she claimed to
be addicted. Dr. Dillon obliged by giving her a vial of half-grain
morphine tablets.

On March 15, Emma LeDoux and Albert McVicar were in Jamestown, where they registered at a hotel as man and wife. Albert was soon back at work at the Rawhide, while Emma told everyone she encountered that she and her husband planned on renting a property and making the town their home. However, within days, their plans appeared to have changed. That was when Albert quit his job and drew all of the money owing to him, a total of $163 in cash. He told his boss that the reason for his sudden resignation was so that he could take up a position as manager of his mother-in-law's farm.

On March 23, the couple was back in Stockton, where they again called at Breuner's furniture store and purchased additional items. Emma also made a change to the delivery instructions. The furniture was now to be delivered to her mother's address, care of Mr. Eugene LeDoux, who she said was her brother-in-law. That evening, she and Albert again checked into the California Hotel, where it appeared that they were in the mood to party. Albert was seeing carrying three flasks of whiskey up to their room at 9:15 p.m. He would not leave that room alive.

The next morning, Emma LeDoux went to a local retailer and bought a large trunk, which she asked to be delivered to room 97 at the California Hotel. She then went to G. H. Shaw's hardware store where she purchased some rope to "tie up a trunk filled with dishes." On her return to the hotel, she encountered porter Charles Berry and asked him to call at her room at 12:15. She had a large trunk that needed to be taken to the rail depot in time for the four o'clock train, she said. Berry arrived as instructed but found that the trunk was too heavy and that he could not lift it on his own. He went to fetch help, returning a short while later with a young man named Joe Dougherty. The two of them then transferred the trunk to the depot where they found a jittery

Mrs. LeDoux waiting. "Why have you taken so long?" she demanded. "I thought that we might miss the train."

The trunk was duly tagged for loading onto the four o'clock train. Satisfied that everything would now proceed as planned, Mrs. LeDoux departed for the Royal House Hotel in San Francisco, where she had an assignation with a young man named Joseph Healy. Healy had met Emma a few months earlier when she had introduced herself as a widow named Emma Williams. He'd quickly fallen for her and had asked her to be his wife. Despite currently being wed to two men, Emma had said yes and gladly accepted his ring. Now she was stringing him along again, declaring her undying love as they snuggled together in their love nest.

But, unbeknownst to Emma, another of her schemes was at that very moment being unraveled. There was trouble at the rail depot. As the trunk was about to be loaded into the baggage car, the baggage master noticed that it was improperly labeled. He therefore ordered it removed and placed on the truck for transport back to the depot.

The heavy trunk, however, aroused suspicion in the railway man. He did not like the weight of it, the balance, the thumping noise from within as it was moved. He also thought that he detected an unpleasant odor and therefore ordered that the trunk be opened. Inside was the body of a man, fully dressed except for his coat and shoes, but decidedly dead. He was soon identified as Albert McVicar. The local coroner would determine that he had died of morphine poisoning.

A detective by the name of Ed Gibson was assigned to the case. And it did not take him long to find out about the rendezvous Emma LeDoux had kept at the Royal House with Joseph Healy. Healy was tracked and brought in for questioning. He said that LeDoux had told her that her husband had recently died in Colorado. The next morning, Healy had a seen a newspaper story about the discovery of McVicar's body in a trunk in Stockton and had pointed it out to her. On reading the story, Emma had said that she needed to get back to Stockton urgently. They'd then gone to the railway station and bought tickets. Healy said that he'd traveled as far as Point Richmond with Emma and had then left the train. He hadn't seen or heard from her since.

That Emma LeDoux hadn't ridden the train all the way to Stockton did not come as a surprise to Det. Gibson. He immediately contacted all stations along the route by telegram and learned that LeDoux had left the train at Antioch and was currently shacked up at the Arlington Hotel in that town, where she was registered as Mrs. Jones. LeDoux was taken into custody that very afternoon and brought back to Stockton. She had a lot of questions to answer.

Emma LeDoux was exceedingly calm and collected when confronted by the detective. She had a ready explanation for how her husband had ended up dead in a trunk, albeit one that Gibson found hard to swallow. According to Emma, she, Albert and a man named Joe Miller had been drinking in their room on the night of March 23. At some point during the evening, Miller had slipped poison into Albert's glass and he'd lapsed into unconsciousness after drinking it and soon died. Miller had then forced her to help him dispose of Albert's body, stating that she would be the prime suspect if the murder were reported to the police. Fearful of arrest, she had agreed to go along with the plan. That was why she'd bought the trunk and arranged for it to be loaded onto the train.

The story might have been more believable if Emma had taken the time to furnish "Miller" with a motive or if she'd been able to prove that he was real and not some figment created to get her off the hook. As it was, all of the evidence pointed to her as the killer, and that was how the Grand Jury ruled when it convened on April 2.

Fifteen days later, on April 17, Emma LeDoux was hauled before the court to answer for her crime. The prosecution had a strong case, including testimony from Joseph Healy, Dr. Dillon, and the porter, Charles Berry. It also presented a compelling motive. LeDoux had been fearful of McVicar uncovering her bigamous marriage to Eugene LeDoux. She'd therefore decided to kill him, but she also had seen an opportunity to fleece him before he died. McVicar was desperate for a reconciliation, so it had been easy to convince him to buy a whole houseful of furniture, items she planned to enjoy with her new husband, Eugene LeDoux. Getting him to quit his job and draw his outstanding pay was also easy. All she had to do was convince him that there was a highly paid position waiting for him on her mother's farm.

LeDoux, still clinging to her ludicrous story about the fictitious Joe Miller, never stood a chance against such an overwhelming case. She was found guilty of murder and sentenced to death by hanging. That sentence would later be overturned on appeal, with a new trial date scheduled for January 26, 1910.

But on the morning that the second trial was due to commence, Charles H. Fairall, Le Doux's attorney, received the following letter from his client, which he subsequently made public:

"Dear Sir,

Owing to the condition of my health, which has become badly shattered by four years of confinement, I do not feel able to stand the strain of another trial.

I therefore have decided to plead guilty, and I want you to do what you can to dispose of the matter quickly.

Yours sincerely,

Mrs. Emma LeDoux."

By writing this letter, LeDoux had chosen to throw herself on the mercy of the court, and it worked to an extent since her original death sentence was downgraded to life in prison. She would serve just 11 years before being paroled in 1921, but that was far from her last run-in with the law. During the next two decades, she was in and out of jail on various offences. She died behind bars on July 6, 1941, at the age of 70.

Scene of the Crime

Joe O'Reilly

It was a curious situation. The murdered woman's husband had invited her parents to meet him at his house where their daughter had been killed. Although they were reluctant at first, he had persuaded them by saying that visiting the crime scene had given him a sense of inner peace. Then, after Jim and Rose Callaly arrived at the house in Naul, County Dublin, Ireland, Joe O' Reilly led them to the bedroom were their daughter, Rachel, had been so brutally bludgeoned to death. Blood-spatters on the walls still bore witness to the horrific crime. "This is what I think happened," O'Reilly said as he launched into a bizarre re-enactment of the crime, flailing his arms wildly as though he were killing Rachel all over again. It was then that Jim and Rose Callaly's suspicions were confirmed. Rachel had not been killed by a burglar as Joe had claimed. He, himself, was the killer.

Joe O'Reilly and Rachel Callaly had first met when they'd worked together at Arnott's department store in Dublin. Joe was 19 at the time and was soon attracted to the tall, attractive blonde who was two years his junior. Rachel, however, did not initially reciprocate his feelings. It would take a dogged pursuit before she eventually agreed to go out with him. Things moved quickly after that, and Joe proposed to Rachel while on vacation in Paris. Two years later, they were married and, in the years that followed, the union was blessed with two sons.

On the face of it, the O'Reillys had the perfect marriage. Rachel was now a stay-at-home mom who absolutely doted on her two boys. Joe was upwardly mobile in his career as an advertising account manager, and if his job sometimes kept him away from home, that was compensated in part by the lifestyle it afforded the family. By now, they'd moved to the quite town of Naul, north of Dublin, which Rachel considered the perfect place to raise children.

However, all was not as it seemed. Although Rachel didn't speak openly about problems in her marriage, her friends had the distinct impression that she was unhappy. Joe, meanwhile, had found a confidant. In a series of exceptionally cruel e-mails to his sister Ann, he complained about Rachel's parenting skills, housekeeping skills and cooking. He described his wife in derogatory terms in these mails and even went so far as to say that she "repulsed" him.

But while Joe appeared to have no problem in demonizing his wife, it wasn't as though he was a paragon of virtue himself. He was, for the most part, an absentee parent, who left home every morning before his sons were awake and returned long after Rachel had put them to bed. And it wasn't as if these absences were always work related. Obsessed with his personal appearance, Joe's early morning departures were to do with his daily visits to the gym. As for his late night returns, they had a different cause altogether. After thirteen years of the marriage, Joe had strayed from the path. He was having an affair.

The woman in question was a work colleague named Nikki Pelley. Starting out as an innocent flirtation, this relationship had quickly become serious. Soon Joe was staying over in Dublin two nights a week, rather than coming home to his family. When Rachel questioned him about this, he blamed pressure of work. In fact, he was spending his time with Nikki. He was also talking to her about making their relationship permanent. The only stumbling block was his children. He was not prepared to leave his marriage without them.

And so to the dreadful events of October, 4, 2004, the day that Joe O'Reilly phoned Rachel's mother, Rose, in a frantic state. He told her that Rachel had not picked the children up from crèche and that he had been unable to reach her on the phone despite several attempts. He asked Rose to go to the house to check on her, and it was thus Rose who had the misfortune of finding her daughter's body.

Rachel was lying on the floor of her bedroom in a pool of blood. She had been savagely bludgeoned to death, the blows delivered with such force that they had rendered her almost unrecognizable. Such was the ferocity of the attack that blood had been spattered on the walls, reaching almost to the ceiling. An autopsy would later determine that Rachel's skull was fractured in two places. It was a savage, savage murder.

The initial theory was that Rachel had walked in on a burglar and had then been attacked. There had recently been a spate of robberies in the area. Perhaps Rachel O'Reilly had been the one unlucky householder who had walked in on the criminals, a case of wrong place, wrong time. But even in the early stages of the investigation, the Garda (Irish police) began to wonder about that theory. The house had, indeed, been ransacked. But Rachel's handbag, containing nearly 400 euros was untouched, and there was another 800 euros stashed in a kitchen drawer which had not been taken. What kind of a burglar leaves behind such easy pickings?

Of course, when a murder victim is married, the police always look closely at the surviving spouse as a potential suspect. But Joe O'Reilly appeared to have an unbreakable alibi. He admitted that he and his wife had argued the previous evening and said that he had slept that night in a spare room. He'd left the house at 5:30 that morning, as was his usual habit. He'd not seen Rachel before he departed, but that wasn't unusual. In any case, he'd seen nothing untoward. The house was in an orderly state when he'd left. This version of events was backed up by a work colleague who said that he had met with Joe at the gym early that morning.

O'Reilly's whereabouts for the rest of the morning also appeared to be accounted for. He had left the office at around 7:40 and gone to an on-site meeting with a client at a local bus depot. Later, he was joined at that meeting by the colleague who had met him at the gym earlier that morning. It was while driving back to the office from the meeting that O'Reilly had received the call saying that Rachel had not picked up the children from nursery school.

As far as alibis go, this one seemed solid. But still the police wanted to know more from O'Reilly. What was his relationship with Rachel like? O'Reilly said that it was good, that they argued occasionally but never over anything serious. Had he or Rachel ever been involved in a relationship outside the marriage? He said that he wasn't aware of any infidelity on Rachel's part and insisted that he had never been unfaithful. Later, after continued probing by detectives, he admitted to his affair with Nikki Pelley, although he described it as a "casual fling" that was now over.

Perhaps O'Reilly thought that coming clean about the affair with Nikki would allay police suspicions. But he had underestimated the value that detectives attribute to motive. Previously, they'd struggled to understand why O'Reilly might have wanted his wife dead. The presence of a mistress answered that question. Suddenly, O'Reilly's cold, unemotional acceptance of his wife's brutal death made sense. The police now obtained a search warrant for O'Reilly's computer and learned that his relationship with Rachel was far from the happy one that he had described. Those e-mails to his sister Ann had come back to haunt him. So, too, had the admission of his affair with Nikki Pelley. It did not take a genius to work out that it was far more serious than the "casual fling" O'Reilly had described.

And then came that bizarre demonstration that O'Reilly gave to Rachel's parents at the murder scene. In fact, O'Reilly had offered several of his dead wife's friends and family a visit to the crime scene, so that he could demonstrate his theory of what had happened. He'd appeared disappointed when they had declined. This odd behavior would turn the spotlight of suspicion firmly on him.

There was, however, one small detail that appeared to exonerate O'Reilly – his alibi. It just did not seem possible that he could have traveled from Dublin to Naul, committed the murder, and then returned to Dublin without his absence being noticed. However, as any homicide investigator will tell you, alibis are often smoke and mirrors rather than substance. This was certainly true in the O'Reilly case.

Under scrutiny, it turned out that the alibi was not quite as solid as it had at first appeared. The colleague who had provided the alibi had been mistaken on certain timings and details. A far more accurate picture emerged once the police started examining O'Reilly's cell phone records and viewing CCTV footage from traffic cameras and other sources.

Cellular mast information showed that O'Reilly had not headed directly to the client meeting at the bus depot as he'd claimed. He'd first driven north, towards his home in Naul. CCTV cameras had picked him up at several locations along the route. At around 9 o'clock, he'd taken a call from his lover, Nikki Pelly. That call was routed via a cellular mast that placed him in the vicinity of his house. The next clue we have as to what happened that morning came at 9:40, when Rachel's vehicle was picked up on CCTV driving in the direction of the O'Reilly residence. By then, her husband was probably waiting for her inside. By the time he took his next phone call, just after 10, he was headed back to Dublin and Rachel was lying dead on her bedroom floor.

It was a compelling circumstantial case. Joe O'Reilly, however, wasn't about to give in so easily. He continued to protest his innocence. He even appeared on television to appeal to the killer to give himself up. In another bizarre turn, he invited the media gathered outside his house to come in and film the spot where his wife had been killed. His creepy fascination with the crime scene appeared undiminished.

And yet, despite the evidence against him, Joe O'Reilly remained at large for nearly two years. To the casual observer, it must have appeared that he had gotten away with murder and that the Garda had lost their appetite for prosecuting the case. Nothing could have been further from the truth. Aware that their case was purely circumstantial, the police were biding their time, checking and rechecking every detail, ensuring that when charges were brought, they would stick. Eventually, they were ready to move.

In November 2006, Joe O'Reilly was arrested and charged with the murder of his wife, Rachel. His trial began in June 2007 at the Central Criminal Court in Dublin. There, the jury found that the evidence was compelling enough to warrant a guilty verdict. O'Reilly was sentenced to life in prison. He has subsequently filed several appeals, all of which have been unsuccessful. O'Reilly continues to claim that he is innocent and refuses to express remorse for his crime. That means, of course, that he is ineligible for parole.

The Good, the Bad, and the Deadly

This is the story of three people, three deeply flawed individuals on a collision course with murder, three pawns in a game of jealousy-inspired homicide. This is the story of a good wife, a philandering husband, and a spurned mistress determined to have her way even if she had to kill for it. This is a cautionary tale about the dangers of sexual obsession, a real-life *Fatal Attraction* that happened in Lake Orion, Michigan, in 1999.

Gail Garza had been born in a small Texas town and brought up in a family that was devoutly Catholic. She was a pretty girl, dark-haired and with exotic looks that gained her many admirers. For Gail, though, there was only one boy that she was interested in. Almost from the moment she met George Fulton, she knew that she wanted to share her life with him.

It helped, of course, that George was also Catholic and that he was handsome and athletic and ambitious. He planned on a career as a military officer and had been accepted into United States Military

Academy at West Point. Gail, too, had ambitions. After school, she went off to college and eventually obtained a degree in speech therapy. Then, after four years of managing a long distance relationship, the couple was reunited. Those years had done nothing to dull the flames of their love, and they were married soon after.

Gail Fulton now settled into the lifestyle of a military wife, moving from base to base as her husband was assigned and reassigned. These were relatively happy years, during which the couple had three children and spent time stationed in Germany, Panama, and various locales in the United States. But cracks appeared in the marriage early on, thanks in large part to George's roving eye. Gail tried to ignore his many dalliances, turning to her faith for respite. But the humiliation of it wore her down. She flew home early from the Panama assignment, returning to the bosom of her family in Texas. Thereafter, she suffered a nervous breakdown, was plagued by depression, and lost an alarming amount of weight. And yet, when George showed up, full of contrition and promising that it would never happen again, Gail immediately took him back. This was to form a pattern over the years that followed, a pattern that would end in tragedy.

In 1993, George retired from the Army, filling Gail with hope that they might eventually settle down to a normal life in Texas, close to her family. But George had other plans. He told Gail that he was moving the family to Michigan, giving no reason nor room for discussion on the matter. Gail, the ever dutiful wife, was not about to argue anyway. She was the type of woman who followed the old-fashioned wedding vows. She believed in obeying her husband in all things.

And so, the Fultons packed up their belongings and trekked halfway
across the country to settle in Lake Orion, a small town on the
outskirts of Detroit. She wasn't exactly happy here, especially since
her oldest daughter had stayed behind in Texas to attend college. But
Gail made the best of a bad situation. She found work at the Lake
Orion public library, started attending a local Catholic church and
settled in to doing what she'd always done, supporting her husband
and children. George had at this point started a job that involved a lot
of travel. He was often away from home, and Gail feared that he might
be cheating on her while he was on the road. She prayed hard to
expunge those thoughts from her mind, but the effects of her anxiety
were plain for all to see. Gail had started losing weight again and she
appeared deeply unhappy.

It was during one of George's business trips to Florida that he visited a
bar and met the third player in this melodrama, an attractive brunette
named Donna Kay Trapani. Donna was vivacious and outspoken, quite
the opposite of timid Gail. George spent most of that first evening
trying to seduce her, but Donna appeared disinterested until right at the
end, when she agreed to dance with him. Then they exchanged phone
numbers and, on George's next visit to the Sunshine State, they ended
up in bed together. It was the beginning of a steamy affair.

Donna Kay Trapani was born in Louisiana and raised in poverty by her
single mother. As a child, she was overweight and dowdy, something
that resulted in her being teased and bullied by her peers. Despite these
difficulties (or perhaps because of them), she grew to be a determined
young woman. She did well at school and thereafter registered at
nursing college, eventually earning her degree. In the meantime, she'd
had bariatric surgery to reduce the size of her stomach, and the results
were quite dramatic. With diet and exercise, she trimmed down
considerably, gaining a voluptuous figure to go with her pretty face.

She was suddenly being asked out on dates for the first time, and
Donna indulged fully. Eventually, she married aircraft mechanic,
Charles Trapani, and moved with him to Fort Walton Beach, Florida.

But Donna's ambitions ran far deeper than being a nurse and a
mechanic's wife. Having been raised with nothing, she hankered after
the finer things in life and decided that the only way she was going to
get what she wanted was to go into business for herself. Her idea was
to start an employment agency that hired out nurses to hospitals on
short term contracts. Thus was her company, Concerned Care Home
Health, born.

On the surface, the business model was a solid one. Nursing skills are
in short supply, and there is always a ready market for them. But
Donna was no businesswoman. She was a tyrant who harassed and
terrorized her staff. She'd walk into the office, slamming doors and
file cabinets, sniping and shouting at anyone who crossed her path.
Her employees loathed her, but Donna was on somewhat better terms
with the young nurses on her books. She could often be found holding
court with a gaggle of them at one or other local bar. Charles Trapani,
meanwhile, remained at home.

George Fulton was several months into his relationship with Donna
Trapani when disaster struck. The company he was working for was in
financial trouble, and George found himself out of a job. That meant
no more trips to Florida, no more nights cozying up with Donna in
some motel room. Fortunately, Donna had a solution. She hired
George as Chief Financial Officer in her business, CCHH. Now
George had even more reason to travel down south. George even
relocated to Florida in May 1998, telling Gail that he needed to be

closer to the company head office. In fact, he had moved into a rented apartment with Donna. Back in Lake Orion, Gail fretted over her errant husband and even threatened suicide. It made no difference to George. He was living his version of the perfect life – a sexy mistress to indulge his desires in Florida and a reverent, obedient wife waiting for him back in Michigan.

But George was soon to realize that the occasional weekend fling with Donna and cohabitating under the same roof as her were different things entirely. Donna was a difficult woman to live with, moody, snide and willful. It wasn't long before he was thinking about getting out of the relationship and returning to the arms of the woman who truly loved him. In the spring of 1999, he did just that. As always, Gail took him back with open arms.

Donna, of course, was enraged by this desertion. She was used to getting her own way and determined to win her lover back. George had barely arrived back in Michigan when there was a letter, purportedly from a Florida doctor. According to this note, Donna was pregnant. Not only that, but she had also been diagnosed with terminal cancer. (Both of these claims were a lie; Donna had written the note herself, on stolen stationery.)

Now followed one of the most bizarre episodes of this entire story. On July 2, 1999, George flew Donna up to Michigan and checked her into a hotel. The following morning, he drove Gail to the hotel, telling her that there was someone he wanted her to meet but providing her with no other details. Gail suddenly found herself in a hotel room meeting a woman who George explained to her was expecting his child. Quite understandably, she ran from the room crying.

You might have expected that George Fulton would have gone after his wife, especially since she had in the past threatened suicide over his many infidelities. But in typically callous fashion, he stayed behind with Donna, spending the night with her before ending the relationship the following morning. Then he headed back home to the dutiful Gail.

But George should have known Donna Trapani's character far better by now. Over the weeks that followed, she inundated him with a torrent of phone calls, letters, and emails. She also left several messages on his home phone, where she vented her bile against Gail. When none of that worked, she moved on to another, deadlier plan to win her man back.

Sybil Padgett was an employee of Trapani's, a chubby bottle blonde with a drug habit and a slavish devotion of her employer. When Trapani first voiced the idea of murdering Fulton, the 38-year-old Padgett hinted that her boyfriend, 19-year-old Patrick Alexander, might know someone who could do the job. That "someone" turned out to be 32-year-old Kevin Ouelette, a local thug who fancied himself as a hitman and liked to dress all in black. A fee of $20,000 was agreed upon. On October 3, 1999, Padgett, Alexander, and Ouelette set off for Michigan in a hired Chevy Malibu. The following evening, they were parked outside Gail's place of work, the Lake Orion public library.

Gail Fulton was the last person to leave the library that night, locking up as she left the building. She paid no attention to the only other car in the parking lot, got into her own vehicle and started it up. She'd covered only a few yards, however, before she realized that something was wrong. Pulling the car to the curb, she got out and checked the tires. The front passenger tire was flat.

This, of course, was all part of the killer's plan. Earlier, Patrick Alexander had slashed the tire in order to force Gail to stop. Now, as Gail stood looking down at the damage, Kevin Ouelette got out of the Chevy, crossed the short distance to his victim, raised the gun and fired four shots. Gail was hit in the face, chest, and shoulder. She collapsed to the tarmac, even as Ouelette walked casually away. Moments later, the Chevy drove out of the lot, leaving Gail Fulton to bleed to death on the pavement.

Trapani was ecstatic at the success of her hit team. But she'd made the grave mistake of hiring a bunch of rank amateurs for the job. What Padgett and Co. had failed to notice was that the parking lot was covered by a surveillance camera. The entire murder had been captured on film. All the police had to do was track the rental car back to the man who'd hired it – Patrick Alexander. In the meanwhile, officers had also quizzed George Fulton, and he'd admitted his affair with Donna Trapani, adding that he believed Donna might be behind his wife's murder. There was also another source giving police this same piece of information. Sybil Padgett had told a friend of hers about the murder and that friend had told the police.

Sybil Padgett, Patrick Alexander and Kevin Ouelette were all brought in for questioning. So, too, was Donna Trapani. Under interrogation, Donna denied any involvement in Gail's murder. Unfortunately for her, her co-conspirators were much more forthcoming. Padgett and

Alexander quickly cracked under interrogation while Ouelette didn't even bother trying to deny his involvement. He admitted that it was he who'd pulled the trigger and bemoaned the fact that Donna had stiffed him on the fee they'd agreed.

Donna Trapani was convicted of first-degree murder in December 2000 and sentenced to life in prison without parole. Padgett and Ouelette received similar sentences while Alexander was allowed to plead to second-degree murder in exchange for his testimony against the other accused. He is eligible for parole in 2020.

Sad but True

Ronald True was born an illegitimate child at a time when children born out of wedlock faced a harsh and uncertain future. By the conventions of the age, he could expect to be ostracized by his peers, labeled a bastard and looked down upon. The only reason that young Ronald escaped this fate was because his mother was a pretty sixteen-year-old who attracted the attention of a wealthy young man from a good family and later married him. Ronald never knew his real father, but he grew up in the bosom of the True clan and had their family name to give him respectability. The family's wealth also ensured that he attended the best public schools and never wanted for anything during his childhood.

From an early age, however, there were signs that not all was right with Ronald. He was an intelligent enough boy but prone to odd behavior and to pranks that went beyond mere mischievousness. Those eccentricities followed him into his teens and young adult years. Ronald had opted not to attend university, but his family had nonetheless found a position for him with a respectable private bank. He lasted barely a week before his odd behavior resulted in his dismissal. His next few jobs were of equally short duration before his family decided that some time abroad might help mature him. But he fared no better in the colonies. After disastrous short term appointments in New Zealand and Canada, he ended up in Mexico and then in China where he developed an addiction to opiates.

True returned to Britain after the outbreak of World War I and, through his family contacts, was accepted as a pilot in the Royal Flying Corps. But the Corps soon tired of his propensity for crashing aircraft. After three of its valuable machines were lost through True's recklessness, he was invalided out of the service on "medical grounds." In 1916, he moved to the United States where he used his flight experience to get work as a test pilot and flying instructor. He also married an American woman and fathered a child by her, only to abandon his young family in 1918. His next move was to Ghana, where he was assistant manager of a gold mine for a time.

By the time True returned to Britain a year later, his already unpredictable behavior had deteriorated still further. He was now showing increasing signs of paranoia and was convinced that he had a doppelgänger who was trying to destroy him and claim his identity. Since his mental issues made it impossible for him to hold down a job, his family gave him an allowance, and True lived a life of leisure, visiting the theater, indulging his drug habit and visiting prostitutes. When his allowance proved inadequate to finance these pursuits, he became a conman, using his refined manners and posh public school accent to commit swindles up and down the country.

Olive Young was a 25-year-old prostitute who serviced her clients out of her basement apartment at 13a Finborough Road, in Earl's Court,

London. Olive's real name was Gertrude Yates and she'd once worked as a shop assistant for a West End furrier. But she'd since learned that she could put her good looks to more profitable use as a "lady with male friends," as she put it. Her apartment, in a nicer area of town, was expensive at 43 shillings per week, but Olive's regular roster of wealthy clients meant that she could afford it. There was even enough to pay for a full-time maid, a young woman named Emily Steel.

The first time that Olive encountered Ronald True was on Saturday, 18 February 1922, when he paid to spend the night with her. True was very much like her other clients, genteel, well-spoken and obviously educated. At 31, he was younger and more handsome than most of the gentlemen she entertained, but still Olive didn't like him. There was something odd about True, something that she couldn't quite put her finger on but which frightened her nonetheless. By the time he left the next morning, she had decided that she wouldn't see him again. Her decision was validated soon after when she checked her purse and discovered that £5 had been stolen from it.

But True was not about to give in that easily. His night with Olive had left him infatuated. Over the next twelve days, he tried desperately to set up another date with her. When his phone calls went unanswered, he took to waiting outside her apartment. He begged her for another chance, but Olive remained unmoved, steadfastly refusing his overtures.

At around this time, Ronald True's family was trying desperately to get in touch with him. After years of denials, they had finally admitted to themselves that Ronald was insane, perhaps dangerously so. They had also decided that he belonged in a hospital where he could receive long-term treatment for his mental illness. Sadly, they were unable to track him down before the night of Sunday, 5 March 1922.

That was the night that Olive Young returned from a trip to Piccadilly Circus and found True again standing outside her apartment. It was 11 p.m. and drizzling steadily. Olive had also had a few drinks, and it was perhaps that, along with True's drenched and rather pathetic appearance, that swayed her. She agreed that he could come inside. That turned out to be a tragic mistake.

The following morning, Olive Young's maid let herself into the apartment as normal and encountered True on his way out. "Don't disturb Miss Young," he told her. "We were up late last night, and she is still in a deep sleep."

Emily Steel adhered to that instruction for several hours until she became concerned about her employer and went to check on her. She found Olive, lying on the floor of her bedroom, battered to death with a rolling pin which lay nearby, encrusted with blood. The motive was quite obviously robbery since the victim's purse and jewelry were missing. Even the pile of coins that Olive Young kept to feed the gas meter had been stolen.

There was only ever one suspect. Ronald True was arrested later that night at the Hammersmith Palace in King Street, where he was watching a music hall show. His trial opened at the Old Bailey on Monday, May 1, 1922, with his defense offering a plea of "not guilty by reason of insanity." During the four day proceedings, prosecutor Sir Richard Muir contended that while True undoubtedly had mental issues, he did not meet the criteria for insanity stipulated under the M'Naghten Rules. "He knew what he was doing and knew that it was wrong," Muir argued, and the jury agreed. True was found guilty and sentenced to death.

It was at this point that the True case took a turn that would establish it as a landmark of the British justice system. Five days before True's first appearance in court, another capital case had been put to a London jury. Henry Jacoby, a simple-minded boy of 18, had appeared at the Old Bailey charged with the murder of 65-year-old Lady Alice White. Lady White had been attacked and beaten to death with a hammer while she was a guest at Spencer's Hotel in Portman Square, London, where Jacoby worked as a pantry boy.

There was never any doubt that Jacoby was guilty, but the jury had nonetheless made a strong recommendation for mercy on account of the youth's obvious mental issues. The trial judge had ignored that recommendation and had sentenced Jacoby to death. Despite a petition to the Home Office containing several hundred signatures, the sentence of the court had been carried out on June 5, 1922.

Now, Home Secretary Edward Shortt was faced with a similar decision in the case of Ronald True and, inexplicably, he reached a different decision. True was reprieved from the gallows and committed to Broadmoor Hospital for the Criminally Insane.

Shortt's decision sparked a massive public outcry, adequately fanned by the popular press. The popular perception was that there was one law for the rich and well-connected and another for the working classes. So heated were these protests that a parliamentary committee was formed to examine the law relating to insanity. Ultimately, however, the committee left the M'Naghten Rules of 1843 unchanged.

Not that any of this affected Ronald True's sentence. He would remain incarcerated at Broadmoor until his death in 1951, at the age of 60. While in prison, True became an inmate impresario of sorts, organizing plays and other entertainments for his fellow prisoners. Those who knew him said that he appeared to have found his calling at last.

Boys Don't Cry

Shortly after 10 a.m. on the frigid morning of December 31, 1993, Anna Mae Lambert pulled her car to a stop in front of the ramshackle farmhouse that her daughter, Lisa, rented in Richardson County, Nebraska. Anna Mae was there to drop off some things for Lisa and her 8-month-old son, Tanner, but immediately she noticed that something was wrong. The front door stood open which seemed unusual on such a bitterly cold day. Entering the house, Anna Mae spotted an African-American man sitting on the floor with his back to the couch. Then she heard her grandson crying in the bedroom and hurried down the passage towards him.

Entering the room, Anna Mae went directly to Tanner's crib and picked him up. It was then than she noticed water on the floor and turned to see her daughter's punctured waterbed. That wasn't what held her attention, though. Lisa was lying on the deflated bed, not moving, and there was blood on her face. And there was another person, dressed in a sweat suit, lying face down on the floor in front of the bed. Anna Mae took all of this in within the fraction of a second.

Then she snatched Tanner into her arms and ran to the kitchen. It was from there that she called the police.

The call was initially fielded by the Richardson County Sheriff's Department who relayed it to the Humboldt Rescue Squad at around 10:20 a.m. A team, under Deputy Ray Harrod, then raced to the farmhouse, picking up a local doctor on route. The information they had was scant at this time, but Harrod knew that this was a potential crime scene. Immediately on arrival, he instructed his team to secure the perimeter. Then he entered the house.

The first thing that Harrod saw was a young African-American man slumped against the couch, a coffee table pulled over his lap. He could see immediately that the man was dead. There was a bullet wound to his jaw that exited on the right side of his head. A suicide? Harrod wasn't sure, but the absence of a gun at the scene suggested otherwise.

Directed by Anna Mae Lambert, Harrod next proceeded to the bedroom where he found the other two victims, a blonde woman in her early twenties and a baby-faced young man with brown hair. Both appeared to have been shot execution style. Harrod had no idea who they were, but Anna Mae stoically identified the blonde as her daughter, Lisa. Then Richardson County Sheriff, Charles Laux, arrived to clear up the other half of the mystery. The young "man" was actually a woman, 21-year-old Teena Brandon. Laux had interviewed her just a week earlier after she'd reported that two local miscreants, John Lotter and Tom Nissen, had raped her at a Christmas party.

Based on the condition of the bodies, the officers were certain that Teena Brandon had been the primary target of the killers. Teena had been stabbed in the abdomen, bludgeoned with some heavy object, and then executed at close range with the gun placed under her chin. The other two victims had been shot, each suffering two bullet wounds at close quarters. This, the officers believed, had been done to prevent them identifying the killers.

Richardson County is, in general, a low-crime area. Homicides are rare and the local cops lack the resources to deal with investigations of this nature. Sheriff Laux thus placed a call to the Nebraska State Patrol. A crime scene unit was soon on the scene and just as quickly started picking up valuable clues including tire imprints, shell casings, a footprint, a spent bullet, cigarette butts and spots of blood. A wallet was also found on the male victim, with an ID card that identified him as 19-year-old Phillip DeVine.

With the processing of the crime scene complete, the bodies were removed to the hospital morgue for autopsy. Meanwhile, the Richardson County Sheriff's Department went looking for John Lotter and Marvin Thomas Nissen. They were not that difficult to find, which raises the question of why they were at liberty in the first place, with rape charges hanging over their heads. The truth of it was that Sheriff Laux had never treated Teena Brandon's allegations with the seriousness they deserved. As would later become clear from interview transcripts, Laux regarded Teena with deep suspicion and barely-concealed disgust. It was the kind of prejudice that Teena had lived with all her life.

Teena Renae Brandon was born in Lincoln, Nebraska, on December 12, 1972. She was born and raised a girl but realized early in life that she didn't feel like one. Her gender identity was that of a male, and by high school she was calling herself Billy, dressing as a boy and dating girls from other high schools, passing herself off as male. She even got engaged twice.

But putting up a front was one thing and the internal life of Teena Brandon was quite another. She was incredibly lonely, conflicted and confused with no one to talk to about her feelings. When she tried, she was met with hostility and antagonism, even from some within her own family who considered her a habitual liar.

There was some validity to that. Teena did have a propensity for lying and also for other forms of dishonesty, like forging checks and stealing money. Inevitably those habits got her into trouble, and it was thus, in late 1993, that she decided to seek a fresh start elsewhere, where nobody knew her and where she could pass herself off as a man. The ultra-conservative town of Humboldt, Nebraska, eighty miles south on NE-2, was probably not the best choice for such a re-invention, but that was where Teena headed. By the time she arrived, Teena Brandon had become Brandon Teena.

One of the first people that Brandon met in Humboldt was single-mom Lisa Lambert, who was moonlighting as a bartender at Big Mike's tavern. Lisa was attracted to the handsome, if somewhat girlish, stranger and invited him to stay at her farmhouse. However, Brandon had been in town only a few days when his eye fell on someone else, a pretty 19-year-old named Lana Tisdel. And that attraction was mutual. With his hair clipped short, the five-foot-five, 112-pound Brandon would have passed as a scrawny but otherwise handsome young man in anyone's book.

Dating Lana meant also that Brandon was introduced to some of her friends, including Phillip DeVine, who was going out with Lisa's sister. There was also Tom Nissen and John Lotter. John had once dated Lana and still had a thing for her. Unbeknownst to Brandon, both he and his buddy Tom had served prison time. Still, it seemed that Brandon was accepted into his new circle of friends. He was Lana's new flame and they appeared to be very much in love.

And then came the fateful day of December 15. Brandon, short on money, had fallen back on old habits and tried to cash a forged check. Arrested on that charge, he was locked up in the county jail. Hearing of his arrest, Lana went immediately to visit him. Imagine her confusion when she arrived at the jailhouse and was directed to the women's section.

Lana was horrified by the whole episode, more so when Brandon told her that he was a hermaphrodite – half-male/half-female – and would shortly be undergoing a sex change operation. Yet, to her credit, she stuck by him. Defying her mother on the issue, she arranged for Tom Nissen to bail him out.

In the meanwhile, rumors about Brandon's sexuality had begun circulating among Lana's friends after a local newspaper identified him as a woman in the story covering his arrest. John Lotter, in particular, seemed obsessed with the issue. He openly called Brandon a "freak" and said that he didn't want him anywhere near his former

girlfriend, Lana. Matters escalated at a Christmas party two days later,
where Lotter and Nissen got drunk and then insisted that Brandon
prove his manhood. When Brandon refused they grabbed him, pulled
down his pants and insisted that Lana have a look. She, instead, fled
the house, leaving Brandon at the mercy of the two ex-cons.

Brandon was dragged into a bathroom where he was punched in the
stomach and then kicked after he fell. He was marched from the house
and forced into a car. He was then driven to a secluded spot where the
assault continued. After being beaten into submission, Brandon was
forced to remove his pants and was then raped and sodomized by Tom
Nissen, before Lotter also had his turn. Lotter and Nissen then drove
away, leaving a cut, bruised and deeply traumatized Brandon out in the
cold, without a coat or shoes in the frigid night.

It was Lana who convinced Brandon to report the assault and rape. But
she had no idea of the level of humiliation this would subject him to.
The authorities were less than sympathetic. Sheriff Charles Laux had
never heard of a transsexual before and spent much of his interrogation
asking questions about Brandon's sexual experiences rather than about
the rape. "Why do you make girls think you're a guy?" he asked with
barely concealed contempt. When Brandon refused to answer, he made
a note on the file that the complainant was being "uncooperative."

Eventually, the humiliating process was over and Brandon signed the
complaint and left the police station. He assumed that his attackers
would be arrested, but three days passed without the Sheriff's
department even sending a patrol car out to Tom Nissen's house.
Eventually, on December 28, they were called down to police
headquarters. There Lotter claimed that they had only pulled down

Brandon's pants because Lana had asked them to determine his sex. He insisted that neither he nor Nissen had had sexual relations with Brandon. Nissen was slightly more forthcoming. According to him, Lotter had sex with Brandon, although he claimed that it had been consensual. He and Lotter were then allowed to leave. They would spend the next two days drinking, seething at the "injustice" of being reported to the police. Eventually, on December 30, they went looking for revenge.

It was Lana's mother who directed Lotter and Nissen to Lisa Lambert's farmhouse, where Brandon was staying. Finding the front door locked on arrival, Lotter kicked it open. Then the pair walked down the passage to Lisa's bedroom. They found her in bed and demanded to know where Brandon was. Lisa insisted that Brandon wasn't there, but then Nissen spotted him hiding under a pile of blankets at the foot of the bed and pulled him out into the open. Almost immediately Lotter fired, hitting Brandon in the stomach. Then, as he lay twitching on the floor, Nissen asked Lotter for his knife and used it to stab Brandon several times.

By now, Lisa was screaming. But those screams were snuffed out when Lotter fired at her, hitting her in the abdomen. Then as she collapsed to the bed, Nissen demanded to know if there was anyone else in the house. Lisa said that there was. Phillip DeVine had had an argument with his girlfriend the previous day and was staying over. That proved to be a case of wrong place, wrong time. The young man was dragged into the lounge were Lotter executed him with two bullets. Lotter then walked back to Lisa's bedroom where he finished her off with a bullet that passed through her right eye. All the while, 8-month-old Tanner was just feet away in his crib, screaming in terror and confusion. Lotter left him to cry.

Having carried out the massacre, the killers drove back to Nissen's house in Falls City, discarding their weapons on route. They were arrested that same day, with Nissen informing the arresting officers that it was Lotter who had committed the murders and that he had just been "along for the ride."

Tom Nissen was the first to go on trial, appearing before the courts in February 1995. There, his attorney presented the defense that Nissen had offered from the start. He conceded that his client had been present at the crime scenes but insisted that he had not killed anyone. It was Lotter who had committed the murders.

Unfortunately for Nissen, he had earlier given an interview to Playboy magazine in which he had bragged about raping Brandon and to participating in his murder. That propensity for boastfulness would end up costing him dearly. He was found guilty of first-degree murder in the case of Brandon Teena, and of second-degree murder in the deaths of Lisa Lambert and Phillip DeVine. Sentencing was delayed until after John Lotter's trial, but there was a strong possibility that Tom Nissen would be going to the electric chair.

And the specter of Ol' Sparky appeared to have a galvanizing effect on Nissen. By the time John Lotter's trial began on May 15, 1995, Nissen had switched sides, appearing as the prosecution's star witness against his old buddy. It resulted in a guilty verdict and death penalty for John Lotter. Nissen was subsequently sentenced to life in prison without parole.

The murder of Brandon Teena would have far-reaching consequences. In its aftermath, Brandon's mother JoAnn brought a wrongful death suit against Sheriff Charles Laux and the Richardson County Sheriff's Department. The matter was eventually settled in her favor with the Nebraska Supreme Court ruling that Laux had been negligent in his duty and had been "an essential link in the chain that led to the victim's death." Laux was also castigated by the court for his attitude towards the young rape victim. At one point during the interview, he had referred to Brandon as "it." JoAnn Brandon was awarded $80,000 in damages.

However, the case had a far greater reach than that, highlighting, for the first time, the plight of transgender people. In 1999, it was the subject of a Hollywood movie entitled *Boys Don't Cry*. Hilary Swank won the best actress Academy Award for her portrayal of Brandon Teena in the film.

For more True Crime books by Robert Keller

please visit:

http://bit.ly/kellerbooks

44284733R00085

Made in the USA
Middletown, DE
05 May 2019